£4.25.

Kaleidoscope

An anthology of English varieties for upper-intermediate and more advanced students

Michael Swan

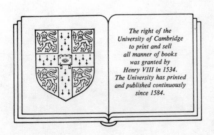

The right of the
University of Cambridge
to print and sell
all manner of books
was granted by
Henry VIII in 1534.
The University has printed
and published continuously
since 1584.

Cambridge University Press

Cambridge
New York   New Rochelle
Melbourne   Sydney

Published by the Press Syndicate of the University of Cambridge
The Pitt Building, Trumpington Street, Cambridge CB2 1RP
32 East 57th Street, New York, NY10022, USA
10 Stamford Road, Oakleigh, Melbourne 3166, Australia

© Cambridge University Press 1979

First published 1979
Eighth printing 1988

Designed by Peter Ducker MSTD

Printed in Hong Kong
by Wing King Tong Co., Ltd

ISBN 0 521 21621 4 Student's Book
ISBN 0 521 23390 9 Teacher's Book

Acknowledgements

The editor and publishers are grateful to the authors, publishers and others who have given permission for the use of copyright material identified in the text. It has not been possible to identify the sources of all the material used and in such cases the publishers would welcome information from copyright owners.

Extracts from *The Oxford Advanced Learner's Dictionary of Current English* by A. S. Hornby are used by permission of Oxford University Press, © OUP 1974; 'Lucy in the Sky with Diamonds', words and music by John Lennon and Paul McCartney © 1967 Northern Songs Ltd, London, England is used by permission of ATV Music; the article entitled 'Paul McCartney and Wings' is reproduced from *The Times* by permission; the extract from *Melody Maker* is by permission; the quotation from the *Penguin Stereo Record Guide* © The Long Playing Record Library Ltd is by permission; the cartoons from Private Eye Productions are by permission; the extract from *Catch-22* is by permission of Joseph Heller and Jonathan Cape; all material from *Punch* is by permission of Punch Publications Ltd; 'Freak's Dream comes True' is from *Truth*, published by Carl Parks and Associates, Spokane, Washington; 'Poem for Roger McGough' © Adrian Henri 1967, and 'Vinegar' © Roger McGough 1967, both from *Penguin Modern Poets 10* and 'At lunchtime a story of love' © Roger McGough 1967, 1974 from *Penguin Modern Poets 10* and the 'Pantomime Poem' © 1971 by Roger McGough from *After the Merrymaking* (Cape) are by permission of Hope Leresche & Sayle; the extract from *The Times* Diary is by permission; all material from Penguin Books is reprinted by permission; the Welsh napkin design is by permission of Fawcett and Lloyd (Textiles) Ltd; the extract from Randolph Quirk, *The Use of English*, is by permission of the Longman Group Ltd; the 'Jargon' article is by permission of *The Daily Telegraph*; the material from the National Insurance Act 1964 is by permission of HMSO; the estimate by Variety Floors Ltd is by permission; all extracts from *The Observer* are by permission; all extracts from the *New Statesman* are by permission; *Superman* by John Updike is published by Victor Gollancz Ltd; the material from *Funny Ha Ha* and *Funny Peculiar* by Denys Parsons and the *Pan Puzzle Book* are by permission of Pan Books; the small ads and articles are by permission of *Time Out;* the extract from Gerald Durrell, *Birds,*

passage by Wole Soyinka is by permission of African Universities Press; the artwork from *The Wizard* and *The Beezer* is by permission of D. C. Thomson & Co. Ltd; the map from *British History Atlas* by Martin Gilbert is by permission of George Weidenfeld and Nicolson Ltd; the army poster is reproduced by permission of the Controller, HMSO, © Crown; the *Mad* cartoon is © 1971 by E. C. Publications Inc; the extract from *Summerhill: A Radical Approach to Child Rearing* by A. S. Neill is by permission © 1960 Hart Publishing Co.; the extract from *Overkill and Megalove* by Norman Corwin is by permission of Harry N. Abrams Inc; the poem by Robert Frost is by permission of Jonathan Cape on behalf of the estate of Robert Frost; the cover and predictions from *Old Moore's Almanack for 1977* are © W. Foulsham & Co. Ltd, reproduced with permission; the extracts from the *Sun* are by permission; the report on horoscopes is reproduced from *Which?* (June 1969) and used by permission of the publishers, Consumers' Association, Copyright; the map from the Wainwright *Guide* is by permission of the Westmorland Gazette; the extract from *The Next Horizon* by Chris Bonington is by permission of Victor Gollancz Ltd; the poem by Carl Sandburg and the excerpt from *Bury my Heart at Wounded Knee* by Dee Brown are by permission of Holt, Rinehart and Winston Ltd; the extract from *A High Wind in Jamaica* by Richard Hughes is by permission of the author's estate and Chatto and Windus; the poem by T. S. Eliot is by permission of Faber & Faber Ltd; the extract reprinted from *The Big Red Diary 1977* compiled by Christine Jackson with information from the National Council for Civil Liberties is published by Pluto Press, London; the extract 'You know what I mean' is by permission of Alkatraz Corner Music Co.; the extract *Film 76* is by permission of BBC Publications; the extract from *Executioner Pierrepoint* by Albert Pierrepoint is by permission of George Harrap & Co. Ltd; the material from *A Hanging* by George Orwell published by Martin Secker & Warburg is by permission of A. M. Heath & Co. © Mrs Sonia Brownell Orwell; the extract from *Rosencrantz and Guildenstern are Dead* by Tom Stoppard is published by Faber & Faber Ltd; the material from *Sanity, Madness and the Family* by R. D. Laing is published by The Tavistock Institute of Human Relations; the extract from *Bank Shot* by Donald Westlake is by permission of Hodder & Stoughton Ltd; the poem by Harry Graham from *Most Ruthless Rhymes* is published by Edward Arnold; the material from *Baby and Child Care* by Benjamin Spock is © Simon and Schuster; the poems from *The People, Yes* by Carl Sandburg, © 1936 by Harcourt Brace Jovanovich Inc., © 1964 by Carl Sandburg, are reprinted by permission of the publishers; 'Not mine' is reprinted from *Prose of Relevance 1*, by Kenneth J. Weber, by permission of Methuen Publications, Toronto; the extracts from Raymond Chandler *Farewell, My Lovely* and *Playback*, published by Alfred Knopf Inc. and Houghton Mifflin respectively are by permission of Hamish Hamilton Ltd

Introduction

Written English is not just literature, newspaper reports and magazine articles. During a typical day our eyes take in an enormous variety of written messages: business letters, bills, advertisements, notices, personal letters, train timetables, parking tickets, bank statements, political slogans, book-jackets, road-signs, shopping lists, graffiti, the labels on beer bottles . . . the list is endless.

One purpose of this book is simply to provide examples of this variety. The student of English abroad can find plenty of 'good writing' in his textbooks, but it is not always so easy for him to get the taste of practical everyday communication in English. It is certainly a fine thing to study Hemingway's prose style or Galbraith's views on economics, but it can also be interesting to see how a London estate agent advertises a house for sale, or what kinds of thing English children find in their comics. The texts reproduced here have therefore been chosen deliberately in order to include as many kinds of communication as possible. They differ widely in subject-matter, purpose, style and visual presentation. Not all of them are in 'standard' English, nor are they all of British or American origin. Although the emphasis is on written communication, there are also a number of transcriptions of spoken language.

A second purpose – equally important – is to entertain, amuse, inform, surprise, move and occasionally shock the reader. As far as possible, I have chosen texts not only because they illustrate certain types of communication, but also because they have some interest in themselves, either alone or in combination with the texts that come before and after them. Each extract is linked with the next by some kind of association (for instance, similarity of subject-matter or style). The book has the same loose organization as a 'train of thought', and wanders, not very systematically, over perhaps forty or fifty topics. There is no need to start at the beginning or read from left to right: the book is meant to be picked up, dipped into, put down, and (I hope) picked up again later. Brief vocabulary explanations are provided as a quick aid to reading; they should not of course be regarded as complete explanations of the meaning or use of the words explained.

I have tried to provide a reasonably balanced selection of subjects and attitudes, so that the book should contain something for everybody. Obviously, any collection of this kind is personal, and must to some extent reflect the editor's tastes, interests, and political and social concerns. No one person can be expected to share all my likes, dislikes and enthusiasms: I hope at least that most readers will enjoy most of the texts.

A number of people have helped me with suggestions, advice and criticism: I should like to thank all of them, and particularly H. A. Swan, Claire Boasson, Stuart Hagger and my wife.

Note for teachers

A collection of short authentic texts like this is obviously particularly suitable for extensive reading practice outside the classroom. However, it can also be used as a basis for various kinds of classwork. Examples of possible activities are:

Class discussion: a text or group of texts can be used as a jumping-off point for discussion of the writer's ideas and attitudes.

Lecturettes: individual students can each choose a text and tell the rest of the class about their reactions to it.

Vocabulary study: students can work intensively on the words and expressions contained in a text, distinguishing (with the teacher's guidance) between items that are useful for recognition only and items that can become part of their active vocabulary.

Guided composition: students can practise writing in the same style as the text, or using the vocabulary of the text to express their own ideas on the subject.

Stylistic analysis: a class can discuss the style of a particular passage, or compare the styles of different texts on the same subject.

Background study: texts can provide a useful basis for discussion of British and American cultural attitudes, institutions, etc.

To my mother,
who likes anthologies.

Kaleidoscope

, the 11th le.

,ſ/ *n* ⚠ (colloq) (offeι.
ᵖerson.
.ᵊ(r)/ *n* Emperor (esp of Germany
.ɓ).

.ıono /ˈkækıˈməʊnəʊ/ *n* Japanese painting
.ᴜ hanging scroll of silk or paper.

ᴋale, kail /keıl/ *n* kind of curly-leaved cabbage.

ka·leido·scope /kəˈlaıdəskəʊp/ *n* [C] **1** tube containing mirrors and small, loose pieces of coloured
glass. When the tube is turned, constantly changing patterns are seen through the eye-piece. **2** (fig)
frequently changing pattern of bright scenes: *Sun-
light and shadow made the landscape a ~ of colour.* **ka·leido·scopic** /kəˈlaıdəˈskopık/ *adj*
quickly changing.

kal·ends /ˈkælendz/ *n pl* ⇨ calends.

kam·pong /ˈkæmpoŋ/ *n* (in Malaysia) eˈ
space; village.

kan·ga·roo /ˈkæŋgəˈru/ *n* Australiˈ
that jumps along on its stronɡ
female has a pouch in which ı·
⇨ the illus at large. **~ cᴄ**
authority by workerѕ
someone whom thˈ
against their interˈ

kao·lin /ˈkeıəˈ
making poˈ

ka·pok
(froˈ
cˈ

kaⱼ
coveι
covereᴜ

ke·bab /kᴄ
small pieceѕ
skewers.

ked·gerᴇ
eggs

keˈ

(*Oxford Advanced Learner's Dictionary of Current English*)

I

Lucy in the Sky with Diamonds

Picture yourself in a boat on a river with tangerine trees
And marmalade skies.
Somebody calls you, you answer quite slowly, a girl with
    kaleidoscope eyes.

Cellophane flowers of yellow and green, towering over your head.
Look for the girl with the sun in her eyes and she's gone.

Lucy in the sky with diamonds. Ah, ah.

Follow her down to a bridge by a fountain where rocking horse
    people eat marshmallow pies.
Everyone smiles as you drift past the flowers that grow so incredibly
    high.

Newspaper taxis appear on the shore, waiting to take you away.
Climb in the back with your head in the clouds, and you're gone.

Lucy in the sky with diamonds. Ah, ah.

Picture yourself on a train in a station, with plasticine porters with
    looking glass ties.
Suddenly someone is there at the turnstile, the girl with
    kaleidoscope eyes.

Lucy in the sky with diamonds. Ah, ah.

Lennon & McCartney

Lucy in the Sky with Diamonds: the initial letters of the title are supposed to be a
reference to the hallucinogenic drug LSD
tangerine: fruit like a small orange
cellophane: transparent material used for wrapping
rocking horse: toy wooden horse that rocks
marshmallow: kind of soft sweet
plasticine: soft material used by children for making models
looking glass: mirror
turnstile: turning gate made of metal bars

Paul McCartney and Wings
Wembley

Clive Bennett

Paul McCartney is surely the most gifted songwriter of the post-war period. No one else captures so expressively the vulnerability of new love or so poignantly the loneliness in our society. He is no less successful using pulsating rock rhythms to express happiness. When his talent is coupled to a real performing skill the result is, and on Tuesday was, unstoppable.

McCartney and his band Wings have been playing their 2½-hour set more or less constantly round the world for the past 13 months. By now they have polished their lighting and stage effects to a rare pitch of excellence and their simple performance style follows suit.

Despite its familiarity, they showed no signs of boredom with their set. In any case, it was too inventive and the audience response too positive for there to be much danger of that. Most of the songs came from McCartney's post-Beatles days, though there was a sprinkling of the older numbers. Significantly, two he performed in his solo spot, "Blackbird" and especially "Yesterday", came from that period and received the loudest applause, and the first piece really to get the audience going was another, "Lady Madonna".

The set was in two parts. The first opened with McCartney appearing Apollo-like from a cloud of dry ice, descending bubbles and simple but effective lighting. It reached a climax 10 songs later with "Live and Let Die", the stage shrouded in a mass of perfectly timed smoke bombs seared by a laser beam. After the applause the band took up their acoustic instruments for a selection of simpler songs before a return to electrical instruments and a scintillating version of "You Gave Me the Answer".

A word of praise for the members of the band. All of them took their solo spots as expected, but the extra highlight was in the backing brass quartet and especially Tony Dorsey, the trombonist.

(*The Times*)

vulnerability: a vulnerable person is easily hurt
poignantly: movingly
coupled to: joined to
pitch: level
follows suit: is the same
a sprinkling: a few
a cloud of dry ice: steam from frozen carbon dioxide
shrouded: covered
seared by a laser beam: with a very intense beam of light (produced by a special physical process) burning through the smoke
acoustic instruments: instruments played without electronic amplifiers
scintillating: sparkling, brilliant

The Sex Pistols

[The Sex Pistols are a punk rock group.]

So the Stones now are the elite of the rock 'n' roll establishment and the Sex Pistols are the new people knocking at the door. They're knocking the Stones, basically. The Stones are the Establishment to them. They're starting from there, or that sort of premise.

A lot of kids of 16 to 18, the Stones and groups of that era don't mean a thing to them. They're too old for a start. They're all over 30, and the kids want some young people they can identify with and maybe don't play so good. (Laughs). I mean, a lot of people criticise the Sex Pistols for not playing that good.

Well, for a start they've only been playing for about eight months anyway, so that's probably a fair criticism technically, but I think a lot of kids watch them and think, " yeah, I could get up there and do that. Let's form a group." Again, that hasn't happened for a long time because groups are too good.

The musicianship is so high that for kids of 16 there was no way they could think, " I can get up there and do that." They'd have to play for ten years, or maybe never do it. But the Sex Pistols are very instant, where anybody could form and have a go.

It may not work, but at least kids are being encouraged to form a group, almost like the youth club syndrome of the Shadows era. Already there's about 12 groups started in London directly inspired by the Sex Pistols.

(From an interview with Nick Mobbs of EMI records, reported in *Melody Maker*)

the Stones: the Rolling Stones pop group
elite: people at the top
establishment: people with power and authority
knocking the Stones: attacking the Stones
premise: basis
era: period
instant: immediate
syndrome: fashion

Sir,—The action of the man who tore up his Guardian (Letters, December 11) in response to reading about the man who smashed his television set while watching the Sex Pistols interview so infuriated me that I stamped on my reading glasses.—

John Flanagan.
16 Daisy Bank,
Quernmore,
Lancaster.

(*Guardian*)

(i) *Les Illuminations* (song cycle), *Op. 18;* (ii) *Serenade for tenor, horn and strings, Op. 31.*

> *** Decca SXL 6449. Peter Pears (tenor), English Chamber Orchestra, the composer; (ii) with Barry Tuckwell (horn).

This superb interpretation of the *Serenade* by Peter Pears appeared first in coupling with Britten's *Young Person's Guide*, but this pairing with the earlier song cycle is clearly more logical. Pears's voice is so ideally suited to this music, his insight into word-meaning as well as into phrase-shaping so masterly, that for once one can use the word 'definitive'. With dedicated accompaniment under the composer's direction and superb recording this is a disc to recommend to all who have yet to discover the magic of Britten's music.

(*Penguin Stereo Record Guide*)

Op. 18: Op. is the abbreviation for the Latin word opus (= work), used in numbering musical works
in coupling with: on the same record as
definitive: the word suggests that this interpretation is 'final'; it could not be improved
have yet to discover: have not yet discovered

THIS WEEK'S
TOP TWENTY

1	YES SIR I CAN BOOGIE	BACCARA
2	BLACK IS BLACK	La BELLE EPOQUE
3	YOU'RE IN MY HEART	ROD STEWART
4	SILVER LADY	DAVID SOUL
5	NAME OF THE GAME	ABBA
6	ROCKIN' ALL OVER THE WORLD	STATUS QUO
7	BLACK BETTY	RAM JAM
8	HOLIDAYS IN THE SUN	SEX PISTOLS
9	I REMEMBER ELVIS PRESLEY	DANNY MIRROR
10	STAR WARS THEME	MECO
11	CALLING OCCUPANTS OF INTERPLANETARY	CARPENTERS
12	NO MORE HEROES	STRANGLERS
13	WE ARE THE CHAMPIONS	QUEEN
14	BEST OF MY LOVE	EMOTIONS
15	2.4.6.8. MOTORWAY	TOM ROBINSON
16	I REMEMBER YESTERDAY	DONNA SUMMER
17	NEEDLES & PINS	SMOKIE
18	WONDROUS STORIES	YES
19	WAY DOWN	ELVIS PRESLEY
20	VIRGINIA PLAIN	ROXY MUSIC

POP SINGLES
OUR PRICE 64p

" I SEE 'THOU SHALT NOT COMMIT ADULTERY' 'S DROPPED TO EIGHTH....."

(Private Eye)

"For this I kept the Ten Commandments?"

(Punch)

7

The Ten Commandments

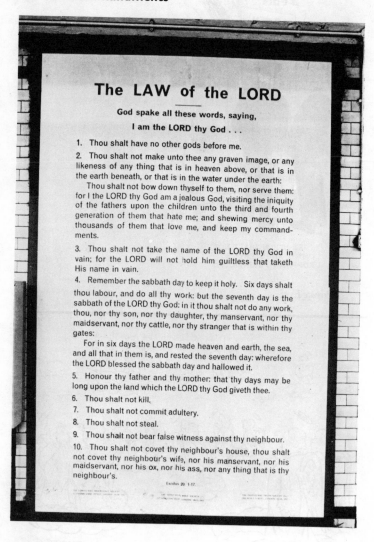

The LAW of the LORD

God spake all these words, saying,

I am the LORD thy God . . .

1. Thou shalt have no other gods before me.

2. Thou shalt not make unto thee any graven image, or any likeness of any thing that is in heaven above, or that is in the earth beneath, or that is in the water under the earth:

Thou shalt not bow down thyself to them, nor serve them: for I the LORD thy God am a jealous God, visiting the iniquity of the fathers upon the children unto the third and fourth generation of them that hate me; and shewing mercy unto thousands of them that love me, and keep my commandments.

3. Thou shalt not take the name of the LORD thy God in vain; for the LORD will not hold him guiltless that taketh His name in vain.

4. Remember the sabbath day to keep it holy. Six days shalt thou labour, and do all thy work: but the seventh day is the sabbath of the LORD thy God: in it thou shalt not do any work, thou, nor thy son, nor thy daughter, thy manservant, nor thy maidservant, nor thy cattle, nor thy stranger that is within thy gates:

For in six days the LORD made heaven and earth, the sea, and all that in them is, and rested the seventh day: wherefore the LORD blessed the sabbath day and hallowed it.

5. Honour thy father and thy mother: that thy days may be long upon the land which the LORD thy God giveth thee.

6. Thou shalt not kill.

7. Thou shalt not commit adultery.

8. Thou shalt not steal.

9. Thou shalt not bear false witness against thy neighbour.

10. Thou shalt not covet thy neighbour's house, thou shalt not covet thy neighbour's wife, nor his manservant, nor his maidservant, nor his ox, nor his ass, nor any thing that is thy neighbour's.

Exodus 20. 1-17.

---

graven: carved
iniquity: sin
take the name . . . in vain: use God's name for purposes that are not serious
hallowed: made holy
adultery: sexual relations between a married person and somebody other than their marriage partner
covet: desire

The God I don't believe in . . .

'And don't tell me God works in mysterious ways,' Yossarian continued.
. . . 'There's nothing so mysterious about it. He's not working at all. He's
playing. Or else He's forgotten all about us. That's the kind of God you
people talk about – a country bumpkin, a clumsy, bungling, brainless,
conceited, uncouth hayseed. Good God, how much reverence can you have
for a Supreme Being who finds it necessary to include such phenomena as
phlegm and tooth decay in His divine system of creation? What in the world
was running through that warped, evil, scatological mind of His when He
robbed old people of the power to control their bowel movements? Why
in the world did He ever create pain?'

'Pain?' Lieutenant Scheisskopf's wife pounced upon the word victoriously.
'Pain is a useful symptom. Pain is a warning to us of bodily dangers.'

'And who created the dangers?' Yossarian demanded. He laughed
caustically. 'Oh, He was really being charitable to us when He gave us pain!
Why couldn't He have used a doorbell instead to notify us, or one of his
celestial choirs? Or a system of blue-and-red neon tubes right in the middle of
each person's forehead. Any jukebox manufacturer worth his salt could have
done that. Why couldn't He?'

'People would certainly look silly walking around with red neon tubes
in the middle of their foreheads.'

'They certainly look beautiful now writhing in agony or stupefied with
morphine, don't they? What a colossal, immortal blunderer! When you
consider the opportunity and power He had to really do a job, and then look
at the stupid, ugly little mess He made of it instead, His sheer incompetence
is almost staggering. It's obvious He never met a payroll. Why, no self-
respecting businessman would hire a bungler like Him as even a shipping
clerk!'

Lieutenant Scheisskopf's wife had turned ashen in disbelief and was
ogling him with alarm. 'You'd better not talk that way about Him, honey,'
she warned him reprovingly in a low and hostile voice. 'He might punish
you.'

'Isn't He punishing me enough?' Yossarian snorted resentfully. 'You
know, we musn't let Him get away with it. Oh, no, we certainly musn't let
Him get away scot free for all the sorrow He's caused us. Someday I'm
going to make Him pay. I know when. On the Judgment Day. Yes, that's
the day I'll be close enough to reach out and grab that little yokel by His
neck and –'

'Stop it! Stop it!' Lieutenant Scheisskopf's wife screamed suddenly, and
began beating him ineffectually about the head with both fists. 'Stop it!'

Yossarian ducked behind his arm for protection while she slammed away
at him in feminine fury for a few seconds, and then he caught her

determinedly by the wrists and forced her gently back down on the bed. 'What the hell are you getting so upset about?' he asked her bewilderedly in a tone of contrite amusement. 'I thought you didn't believe in God.'

'I don't,' she sobbed, bursting violently into tears. 'But the God I don't believe in is a good God, a just God, a merciful God. He's not the mean and stupid God you make Him out to be.'

Yossarian laughed and turned her arms loose. 'Let's have a little more religious freedom between us,' he proposed obligingly. 'You don't believe in the God you want to, and I won't believe in the God I want to. Is that a deal?'

(Joseph Heller, *Catch-22*)

country bumpkin: stupid peasant
bungling: making stupid mistakes
uncouth: uncultivated
hayseed: the same as *country bumpkin*
phlegm: the thick substance that comes up when you cough
warped: twisted
scatological: fascinated by things connected with the lavatory
bowels: lower part of the digestive system
caustically: bitingly, sarcastically
celestial: heavenly
worth his salt: capable of doing a good job
writhing in agony: twisting in terrible pain
blunderer: person who makes stupid mistakes
incompetence: inability to do a good job
staggering: astonishing
met a payroll: had to make money to pay salaries
ashen: grey
ogling him: giving him loving looks
reprovingly: critically
scot free: unpunished
yokel: the same as country bumpkin
contrite: apologetic

Conversion

[An American 'Jesus Freak' (member of an unconventional religious group) talks about his conversion.]

The people I came in contact with every day were bumming me out so much I wanted to scream. Nobody cared about anybody. Nobody had any meaning for their lives and it scared me because I was the same way. One day I was home in my room. I had nothing to do, didn't want to see nobody. Everything was zero. I was just waiting for somebody to bring me a key and unlock me out of my misery . . . I walked over to my window and looked up into the sky and thought 'Why are people so evil? Why am I so burnt out? Why is there always a hassle in my head? Why do I hate? . . . I wondered why I was even in the world in the first place. I didn't have any answers. I just wanted Jesus to take over . . . I said 'Jesus, forgive me. I don't know what to say to you. I don't know anything, but I know you're listening. I'm just tired of hassling in my head.'

After that, my head stopped churning, and I felt calm for the first time. I had a smile on my face. I never used to smile much, but from that day on I've had a smile on my face and my mind's been calm! Before I couldn't talk to people, but now I can talk to anyone – old ladies, kids, anyone.

(*Truth*, the Jesus People's newspaper)

bumming me out: (slang) getting on my nerves
hassle: (slang) disturbance
churning: turning round and round

The 'Lord's Prayer'

Our Father, which art in heaven, hallowed be thy name. Thy kingdom come. Thy will be done in earth, as it is in heaven. Give us this day our daily bread, and forgive us our trespasses, as we forgive them that trespass against us. And lead us not into temptation, but deliver us from evil. For thine is the kingdom, the power and the glory, for ever and ever. Amen.

The god-men say when die go sky
Through pearly gates where river flow,
The god-men say when die we fly
Just like eagle, hawk and crow.
Might be, might be –
But I don't know.

(Australian aborigine description of Christianity)

Vinegar

sometimes
i feel like a priest
in a fish & chip queue
quietly thinking
as the vinegar runs through
how nice it would be
to buy supper for two

Roger McGough

Poem for Roger McGough

A nun in a supermarket
standing in the queue
wondering what it's like
to buy groceries for two.

Adrian Henri

"GOD IS DEAD" - NIETZSCHE

"NIETZCHE IS DEAD" — GOD

(Inscriptions on a wall in Cambridge)

A sermon

[This is taken from the 1960s satirical show *Beyond the Fringe*.]

As I was on my way here tonight, I arrived at the station, and by an oversight I happened to go out by the way one is supposed to come in. And as I was going out, an employee of the railway company hailed me. 'Hey, Jack,' he shouted, 'Where do you think you're going?' That, at any rate, was the gist of what he said. But, you know, I was grateful to him. Because, you see, he put me in mind of the kind of question I felt I ought to be asking you here tonight. Where do you think you're going?

Very many years ago, when I was about as old as some of you are now, I went mountain-climbing in Switzerland with a friend of mine. And there was this mountain, you see, and we decided to climb it, and so, very early one morning, we arose and began to climb. All day we climbed, up and up and up, higher and higher and higher, until the valley lay very small below us, and the mists of the evening began to come down, and the sun to set, and when we reached the summit, we sat down to watch this magnificent sight of the sun going down behind the mountain. And as we watched, my friend very suddenly and violently vomited.

Some of us think life's a bit like that, don't we? But it isn't.

Life, you know, is rather like opening a tin of sardines. We're all of us looking for the key. And I wonder how many of you here, tonight, have wasted years of your lives looking behind the kitchen dressers of this life for that key. I know I have. Others think they've found the key, don't they? They roll back the lid of the sardine tin of life – they reveal the sardines, the riches of life, therein, and they get them out, they enjoy them. But you know, there's always a little bit in the corner you can't get out. I wonder – is there a little bit in the corner of your life? I know there is in mine.

Alan Bennett

oversight: mistake
hailed: called
gist: general meaning
vomited: was sick
kitchen dresser: piece of kitchen furniture which includes cupboards and shelves

Bringing Them Back to Religion

by McMURTRY

'Okay, okay you win!—We'll come to church on Sundays if you stop ringing the bells all night."

"I don't believe I saw you in church on Sunday, Mr. and Mrs. Oakley."

The tower of Babel

Once upon a time all the world spoke a single language and used the same words. As men journeyed in the east, they came upon a plain in the land of Shinar and settled there. They said to one another, 'Come, let us make bricks and bake them hard'; they used bricks for stone and bitumen for mortar. 'Come,' they said, 'Let us build ourselves a city and a tower with its top in the heavens, and make a name for ourselves; or we shall be dispersed all over the earth.' Then the LORD came down to see the city and town which mortal men had built, and he said, 'Here they are, one people with a single language, and now they have started to do this; henceforward nothing they have a mind to do will be beyond their reach. Come, let us go down there and confuse their speech, so that they will not understand what they say to one another.' So the LORD dispersed them from there all over the earth, and they left off building the city. That is why it is called Babel, because the LORD there made a babble of the language of all the world; from that place the LORD scattered men all over the face of the earth.

(Genesis 11, *New English Bible*)

bitumen: black stuff, like tar, derived from petroleum
mortar: the stuff used to stick bricks together
dispersed: scattered
henceforward: from now on
babble: confused speech

A Bath reader says that, browsing in a Japanese bookshop, he found a work called Japanese in Two Weeks. *On expressing doubts about its feasibility, he was shown* Instant Japanese.

(*The Times*)

browsing: looking casually at books in a bookshop
feasibility: possibility

15

Black American English

[A fifteen-year-old lower-class American Negro boy was asked what colour God would be, if he existed. The boy's language is obviously very different from standard educated English. However, this does not mean that it is a less efficient tool for communication – the boy expresses a quite complex idea clearly and effectively.]

INTERVIEWER: Jus' suppose there is a God, would he be white or black?
BOY: He'd be white, man.
INTERVIEWER: Why?
BOY: Why? I'll tell you why! Cause the average whitey out here got everything, you dig? And the nigger ain't got shit, y'know? Y'understan'? So – um – for in order for *that* to happen, you know it ain't no black God that's doin' that bullshit.

(Quoted in Peter Trudgill, *Sociolinguistics*)

you dig?: (slang) you see?
ain't got shit: (slang) has got nothing
bullshit: (slang) nonsense

'I had a vision last night. I saw God.'
'Oh, yes? What's God like?'
'Well, to start with, she's black.'

Jamaican Creole

In Jamaica, standard English is the official language and is spoken there, at the top of the social scale, by some educated Jamaicans and people of British origin. At the other end of the social scale, particularly in the case of peasants in isolated rural areas, the language used is an English-based creole which is not in itself mutually intelligible with standard English. The linguistic differences are great enough for us to be able to say, if these two varieties were the only two involved, that, like Sranan, Jamaican Creole is a language related to but distinct from English. To help make this point, here is an extract from a creole text cited by a Jamaican-Creole scholar, Beryl Bailey:

Wantaim, wan man en ha wan gyal-pikni nomo. Im ena wan priti gyal fi-truu. Im meba laik fi taak tu eni an eni man. Im laik a nais buosi man fi taak tu. Im taat taak tu wan man, bot im get kalops aafta in taak tu di man.

'Once upon a time, there was a gentleman who had an only daughter.

She was a gay and dandy girl. She didn't like to talk to just any man. She wanted a gay, fine man to talk to. She started to talk to a man, but she got pregnant by talking to the man.' (Beryl Bailey's translation is into Jamaican rather than British standard English.)

(Peter Trudgill, *Sociolinguistics*)

creole: mixed language resulting from contacts between Europeans and natives during colonization or trading
is not . . . mutually intelligible with standard English: speakers of these two kinds of English can't understand each other
dandy: pretty

Welsh

[Welsh is not a dialect of English – it is a completely separate language, as different from English as Greek or Iranian. It is related to Scots and Irish Gaelic, and to Breton, spoken in the North-West of France. Welsh is still the first language of a number of people in the country districts of Wales. Here are some Welsh words with their English translations, as illustrated on the paper napkins used in the dining room of a hotel in North Wales.]

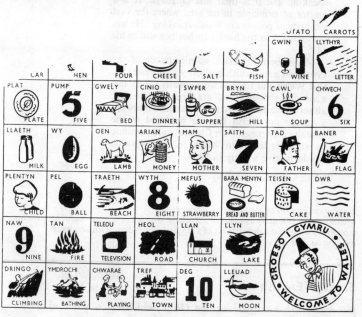

Tit-for-tat Hindi letter irks doctor

A North Wales family doctor was not amused when his letter in Welsh to a local hospital was answered in Hindi.

Dr Carl Clowes, of Llanaelhern, Gwynedd, sent a middle-aged woman patient with a knee injury for x-ray, along with a referral note describing the symptoms, to the Caernarvon and Anglesey hospital at Bangor. The reply, signed by a Dr L.J. Price and written in Hindi, arrived by post.

Dr Price later described the letter as 'a bit of fun'. He was not Welsh-speaking and his two Indian colleagues in the casualty department certainly did not understand Welsh. 'It's a bit of fun really, our way of asking Dr Clowes to write to us in English. We do not always have time to get his letters translated, especially as many nurses do not speak Welsh.'

Dr Clowes is unrepentant. 'This is an insult not only to myself and my patient but to the Welsh language. All my patients are Welsh-speaking and it is their first language. It is a matter of principle in an area where the vast majority of people are Welsh-speaking.' He has complained to the health authorities and to his MP.

Mr Robert Freeman, administrator of the Gwynedd area health authority said yesterday that Welsh and English were equally valid. 'But a lot of our medical staff are English or foreign, although we do try to ensure that there is always a competent Welsh speaker on hand in the casualty department.' Dr Clowes could continue to write his letters in Welsh and in future he would receive a reply in Welsh.

(Ann Clwyd, *Guardian*)

---

x-ray: examination by x-rays (= röntgen rays)
referral note: note sent by a doctor to a specialist who is to examine one of his patients
casualty department: the department of a hospital which deals with accidents
unrepentant: not sorry

Scottish English

[Scotland also has its own language, Gaelic, which is closely related to Irish Gaelic and, more distantly, to Welsh. In addition, Scotland has a number of dialects of English which are very different indeed from the language spoken in England. Here is an old Scottish song, followed by a translation into 'English English'.]

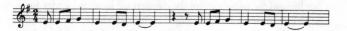

Twa corbies

As I was walking all alane
I heard twa corbies makking mane
That tane until the tither say,
'Where shall we gang and dine the day?'

'In ahent yon old fail dyke
I wot there lies a new-slain knight.
Naebody kens that he lies there
But his hawk and hound and his lady fair.

His hound is tae the hunting gane
His hawk tae fetch the wildfowl hame
His lady's taen anither mate
So we can hae oor dinner sweet.'

There's many an ane for him maks mane
But nane shall ken where he is gane.
O'er his white banes when they are bare
The wind shall blaw for evermair.

Two crows
[Translation into modern standard English.]

As I was walking all alone, I heard two crows complaining.
One said to the other 'Where shall we go and dine today?'

'Behind that old turf wall I know there lies a newly-killed knight.
Nobody knows that he lies there, except his hawk, his hound, and
his beautiful wife.

His hound has gone hunting, his hawk has gone to catch wild-fowl,
and his wife has taken another man, so we can have our good dinner.'

There are many people who mourn for him, but nobody shall know
where he has gone. Over his white bones when they are bare,
the wind shall blow for ever.

Englishes

Of course a scale of styles exists in all our use of English. Each of us works not just with one English but with many Englishes, and the wider the range of our life and the more various the contacts we have, the wider and suppler must be our command over a range of English styles, each of which we know how to use consistently. A haphazard knowledge of several styles may be worse than useless if we do not know the type of occasion on which each is appropriate, or if we do not know when we are sliding from one to another. We do not say, 'It was extremely gracious of you to invite me, Lady Jones, and I've had bags of fun', because 'bags of fun' does not mix with 'extremely gracious', and because to use an expression like 'bags of fun', we should need to know Lady Jones well enough to be addressing her by her first name.

It is not – we must never tire of insisting – that *bags of fun* can be labelled 'bad' or 'slovenly' English, 'a lazy substitute for thought'. 'Bags of fun' is no more a lazy substitute for thought in its appropriate setting than is 'extremely gracious' in the setting that is appropriate for *this* expression. As we have seen repeatedly, it is the height of naïvety to go round with a single yardstick, measuring English as 'good' or 'bad'. Take the opening suggested earlier for an informal letter: 'My dear Frank, it was awfully nice to get your note the other day.' Here are the words that would greatly please the receiver with their warmth and friendliness, yet they include *awfully*, *get* and *nice*, three words which have been condemned so often that many people cannot write them without having a slight feeling of guilt. They have been called 'slovenly' and even 'meaningless'. Such an attitude is plainly ridiculous and can do nothing but harm to the good use of English.

But it would be equally ridiculous to *reverse* the judgement just as flatly. It is the type of judgement that is wrong: it is not merely that the judgement is faulty in this particular instance. If we were studying a review and found the comment 'This is an awfully nice book', our reaction to the words in this situation might well be to call them slovenly and meaningless. We do not want merely polite noises in a review: we want some precise observations about the book's content and quality. Equally, however, we should disapprove of the English used if we were greeted by a friend at a party with the words, 'I apprehend an atmosphere of spontaneous delight with your arrival', whereas 'Awfully nice to see you here' would strike us as just right.

(Randolph Quirk, *The Use of English*)

suppler: more flexible
haphazard: disorganized

slovenly: lazy and careless
yardstick: criterion, standard

Old English

[English is a Germanic language, but since the Norman conquest in the eleventh century it has absorbed a great deal of Latin- and French-based vocabulary, and the grammar has also changed a great deal. Old English – also called Anglo-Saxon – looks like a foreign language to us, and cannot be understood without special study. Here is an extract from a text written by King Alfred towards the end of the ninth century.]

> Forðæm gif ðu swa gewlætne mon metst þæt he bið
> ahweafed from gode to yfle, ne meaht ðu hine na
> mid ryhte nemnan man ac neat. Gif ðu on hwilcum
> men ongitst þæt he bið gitsere ond reafere, ne scealt
> ðu hine na hatan mon, ac wulf.

[Literal translation:]
So if you meet a man so corrupt that he is turned away from good to evil, you may rightly call him not man but animal. If, concerning such a man, you perceive that he is a miser and a robber, you shall not call him man but wolf.

miser: person who is obsessed with money

Foreign English

> In this Competition can to participe
> all people that desire and congregate
> the asking reqierments. Will pass to
> Final all clasificate in the time and
> place asking by the Tecnic Committe.
> In every Race will masculine and
> femenine categories.

(From a notice about a skiing competition in Andorra)

Litel mesteak is not mistak

(Inscription found on a classroom wall in a language school)

21

[If he uses this book] The correspondent will not be compelled to avail himself of obligated periphrase or circumlocutions because of ignorance or forgetfulness of the pertinent word or the opportune phrase at the right moment.

(From the preface to an English–Spanish commercial dictionary)

periphrase, circumlocution: long, roundabout way of saying something (the sentence quoted is a good example)
pertinent: right, appropriate

Jargon

In the Nuts (Unground) (Other than Groundnuts) Order, the expression nuts shall have reference to such nuts, other than groundnuts, as would, but for this Amending Order, not qualify as nuts (Unground) (Other than Groundnuts) by reason of their being nuts (Unground).
(From a government regulation)

For the purposes of this Part of this Schedule a person over pensionable age, not being an insured person, shall be treated as an employed person if he would be an insured person were he under pensionable age and would be an employed person were he an insured person.
(National Insurance Act, 1964, 1st Schedule, Part II)

(Quoted in Randolph Quirk, *The Use of English*)

jargon: unclear language
unground: not ground (to grind is to crush to powder)
groundnuts: peanuts

Royalty terms

During the legal period of copyright the COMPANY shall pay to the AUTHOR:

a) a royalty of 10% on the English published price of all limpbound copies sold but excluding such copies as may by subsequent clauses of this agreement be sold subject to a different royalty;

b) on all copies sold at a special discount of 45% or greater discount a royalty of 10% on the net receipts from such sales;

c) on all copies sold for export at a discount of 45% or greater discount a royalty of 10% on the net receipts from such sales except that copies sold through the American COMPANY shall be exempted from this provision and shall be accounted for in accordance with clause a) or b) as appropriate.

(Extract from a contract between a publisher and an author)

terms: conditions
royalty: percentage of the price of a book paid to the author
limpbound: soft covered
subsequent: following
clause: paragraph of a contract
exempted from this provision: excluded from this condition

Variety Floors Limited

QUOTATION

REE/MEC/1960

Messrs Stuart and George,
421 Banbury Road,
Oxford.

<u>For the attention of Mr Jerome</u>

19th October 1976

Dear Sirs,

<u>Flooring Work</u>

We thank you for your valued enquiry and take pleasure in submitting our quotation as detailed below.

Area & Price

To Rooms 1 & 2 - 65 M2

To supply and lay Heuga (UK) Ltd., Heugaflor 'S' Carpet Tiles.
65 M2 @ £6.66 per M2   £432.90 + VAT

To Rooms, 3, 4, 5, 6, 7, 8, T.V. Room,

To supply and lay Heuga (UK) Ltd., Heugaflor 'S' Carpet Tiles
203 M2 @ £6.66 per M2   £1105 + VAT

Stairs-Hall to 2nd Floor.

To supply and fix Heuga (UK) Ltd., aluminium nosings as necessary.

To supply and fix Heuga (UK) Ltd., Heugaflor 'S' Carpet tiles to treads and risers.

For the sum of   £314.97 + VAT

Doors

To trimming doors to accommodate carpet tiles as necessary.

For the sum of   £2.25 + VAT per door.

The above prices are inclusive of all necessary cutting and waste, and are based on Manufacturers current rates.

Terms

Nett, within 30 days from date of invoice.

We express the hope that the above proves of interest and that your instructions will follow in due course.

Yours faithfully,

R.E. Evans
VARIETY FLOORS LIMITED

quotation: statement of price at which goods or services are offered
M2: square metres
VAT: value added tax
nosings: metal pieces fixed over staircarpet at the front of each stair
tread: horizontal part of a stair
riser: vertical part of a stair
trimming: cutting a little off

A dentist's bill

Telephone
OXFORD 67559

251 ST. JOHN STREET
OXFORD, OX1 2LH

M. Swan, Esq.,
111 Banbury Road,
Oxford

12th August 1976

Mr. F. Walter

presents his compliments and

begs to state that his fee for

Professional Services to the above

date amounts to **Three Pounds**

£ 3 00

I went into a big store in town and asked the assistant for a small packet of washing powder. She handed me a packet marked 'Large'. 'I'm afraid you didn't understand,' I said. 'I asked for a small packet.' 'That's right, madam,' said the assistant. 'It comes in three sizes – Large, Giant and Super. I gave you the small size – Large.'

(Letter in *Competitor's Journal*)

Superman

I drive my car to supermarket,
The way I take is superhigh,
A superlot is where I park it,
And Super Suds are what I buy.

Supersalesmen sell me tonic –
Super-Tone-O, for Relief.
The planes I ride are supersonic.
In trains, I like the Super Chief.

Supercilious men and women
Call me superficial – me
Who so superbly learned to swim in
Supercolossality.

Superphosphate-fed foods feed me;
Superservice keeps me new.
Who would dare to supersede me,
Super-super-superwho?

John Updike

lot: parking place
suds: washing powder
Super Chief: an American long-distance train
supercilious: behaving in a snobbish, superior way
superficial: with no depth of character
superphosphate: a chemical fertilizer
supersede me: take my place

Buy, buy, buy

The most powerful, the loudest and the most persistent command in our society is the command to buy, to consume, to make material progress, to 'grow'. The voice of advertising urges us to buy, buy, buy – and it never lets up. And the voice of advertising is only the most obvious of the forces that include the mass media's portrayal of a way of life in their programmes and stories, the rhetoric of businessmen and politicians praising economic 'progress' and 'growth', and the overwhelming influence of American high schools and colleges in portraying a materialistic way of life as a desirable form of existence, individually and nationally. What are these voices saying? As we seem to hear them, they say, 'Buy', 'Consume', 'Enjoy', 'Grow', 'Advance'.

When advertising paints a picture of consumer hedonism and freedom, and work is considered only a means to that end, the machinery of the Corporate State begins to work towards its own destruction. Consider the hereditary poor. Advertising intended for an audience that can afford what it offers also works (with perhaps even greater effectiveness) on those who cannot afford it; it inflames the desires of the poor without offering them any satisfaction at all. Perhaps the poor are 'better off than they ever were before', but they can hardly be expected to be satisfied after watching television. A continuous display of better living is paraded before them. Rich people know that not every day is filled with sports and glamour; they even know that the person who has everything might not even want all these things. The poor have no way of knowing this; television advertising is far more effective with the unsophisticated. Is there any wonder that we have riots? Television might justly be called a riot box; it raises a fury of dissatisfaction and mocks those who watch it. But even the well-paid, highly motivated executive, after a demanding day, may feel troubled emotions if he views a TV scene of surfers. The screen tells him to work harder so he can vacation in California. But perhaps he senses, in some almost unconscious way, that the harder he works, the less likely it is that he ever will surf; in fact, real surfers don't work at all.

If television is a riot box for the poor, who can say what it is to the ordinary middle-class worker, who has many of the advertised products but lacks the sensuality and freedom they are supposed to bring? The one thing that we can be sure of is that the aim of advertising is to create dissatisfaction, and if the American middle class is still somewhat satisfied, television will keep on trying to subvert it.

(Charles Reich, *The Greening of America*)

lets up: pauses
mass media: newspapers, radio and television
rhetoric: impressive way of talking
hedonism: pursuit of pleasure
Corporate State: the writer's expression for the combination of government and big business which (he feels) rules our lives
surfers: surfing is riding big breaking waves on wooden boards
sensuality: physical enjoyment
subvert it: change its beliefs

Advertisements in a shop window

ROOM TO LET

LARGE BEDSITTING ROOM
AVAILABLE — SUIT QUIET
PROFESSIONAL GENTLEMAN OR
POSSIBLY YOUNG COUPLE. (REFERENCES)
PHONE ALTON 72186

PAIR OF CHAIRS.
£35 PR. GREEN
FARNHAM 69226.

FOR SALE

AIR RIFLE
RAVING BONKERS
FLIGHT DECK
VARIOUS OTHER ITEMS
ALL REASONABLE
FARNAM 21957

SANDERSONS 3 PIECE SUITE COVERS
(CLUB STYLE)   3 SEATER SETTEE +
FLORAL DESIGN   2 CHAIRS.
PERFECT CONDITION. BARGAIN AT £6 THE LOT
WARDROBE MIRROR (42"X10") £5.
(HANGING)
PHONE: FARNHAM 84551 OR CALL
MRS: SMITH   EVENING
14 ANDERSON ROAD
FARNHAM. SURREY.

COUNCIL HOUSE EXCHANGE.

PULBOROUGH SUSSEX,
FOR SIMILAR IN FARNHAM,
OR SURROUNDING AREA
APPLY. MR + MRS BROWN.
10 FARMHOUSE.
FARNHAM 22441

WANTED

FOR PLAYGROUP OPENING IN JAN.
AT THE MALTINGS.
PHONE: 25818.
1 SMALL BEDSIDE CABINET.
1 PIECE CARPET 7ft sq. approx.
1 SMALL WOODEN CLOTHES HORSE.
ANY FARM, ZOO ANIMALS, LARGE
LEGGO, SMALLISH HAMMERS, SAWS etc.

Raving Bonkers, Flight Deck: names of pop records
council house: house built and owned by local government authority
3 piece suite: sofa and two chairs
Leggo: (correct spelling *Lego*) constructional toy

A housewife's shopping list

Co-op
1 tin tomatoes
Water biscuits
Digestive biscuits
Beef Oxo
4 oz. pk walnuts
Self raising flour
Plain flour
Tea
Mustard
Gherkins
Tomato Paste
Yoghurt
Cheeses
Flora
1/2 doz. eggs.

Greengrocer
8 Granny Smiths
1 lb. pears
bananas
satsumas
2 lbs. carrots
2 lbs new potatoes
celery
lettuce
tomatoes
leeks
sprouts
onions
parsley
dates
lemon
1/2 lb. mushrooms

Butcher:
2 lbs. mince
1 1/2 lbs. spice sausages
2 chicken breasts

Boots:
Cling Wrap
Tissues
Colgate

Bakery:
2 Granary cobs

LAUNDRY
COLLECT DRY CLEANING

Oxo: cube for making meat gravy
oz.: ounces
pk.: packet
Flora: a brand of soft margarine
mince: meat ground into small pieces
granary cob: kind of bread loaf
Granny Smiths: kind of apple
Boots: large chain of chemists' shops
Cling Wrap: a brand of transparent paper for keeping food fresh
Colgate: a brand of toothpaste

Things to do

Saturday morning

---

ring ~~Dominique~~

fix journey

~~post~~

photos

accounts

~~phone bill~~

prep. Tuesday teaching

tourist card + check visa position

~~proofs~~

~~flowers~~ ~~Ros Daniels~~

invite Philip + M.

find watch

~~car service~~

crockery

---

proofs: first printing of a book, sent to the author for correction before the final version is published

crockery: cups, saucers, plates etc.

In an ancient volume of Browning's poems at the Donnell Library Center, on West Fifty-third Street, one of our correspondents came upon a memorandum that made his heart, and ours, go out to a lady neither of us is likely to meet – a memorandum that was, in full, as follows:

LONG-RANGE GOALS:
1. *Health – more leisure.*
2. *Money.*
3. *Write book (play?) – fame//// ??*
4. *Visit India.*

IMMEDIATE:
Pick up pattern at Hilda's.
Change faucets – call plumber (who?)
Try yoghurt??

(*New Yorker*)

goals: things to try for; aim at
faucets: (American) water taps
plumber: skilled workman who fits or repairs water pipes, etc.

(Schulz)

31

●HELLO! OBJECTIVE criticism wanted.
I am unheard of writer. I want to be
heard. If you would like to criticise or
commission any of my work please contact
Box No. 123.

(*Time Out*)

commission any of my work: pay me to write

The would-be author

'I've just completed,' said Donald, 'the first chapter of my novel and so we came out hot foot, as it were, so that I could read it to you.'

'Oh, God,' said Larry horrified. 'No, Donald, really. My critical faculties are completely dehydrated at half past two in the morning. Can't you leave it here and I'll read it tomorrow?'

'It's short,' said Donald, taking no notice of Larry and producing a small sheet of paper from his pocket, 'but I think you will find the style interesting.'

Larry gave an exasperated sigh and we all sat back and listened expectantly while Donald cleared his throat.

'Suddenly' he began in a deep vibrant voice, 'suddenly, suddenly, suddenly, there he was and then, suddenly, there she was, suddenly, suddenly, suddenly. And suddenly he looked at her, suddenly, suddenly, suddenly, and she suddenly looked at him, suddenly. She suddenly opened her arms, suddenly, suddenly, and he opened his arms, suddenly. Then suddenly they came together and, suddenly, suddenly, suddenly, he could feel the warmth of her body and suddenly, suddenly, she could feel the warmth of his mouth on hers as they suddenly, suddenly, suddenly, suddenly fell on the couch together.'

There was a long pause while we waited for Donald to go on. He gulped once or twice as though overcome with emotion at his own writing, folded the piece of paper carefully and put it back in his pocket.

'What do you think?' he enquired of Larry.

'Well, it's a bit short,' said Larry, cautiously.

'Ah, but what do you think of the style?' said Donald.

'Well, it's um, interesting,' said Larry. 'I think you'll find it's been done before, though.'

'Couldn't have been,' explained Donald. 'You see, I only thought of it tonight.'

'I don't think he ought to have any more to drink,' said Leslie loudly.

'Hush, dear,' said Mother. 'What do you intend to call it, Donald?'

'I thought,' said Donald, owlishly, 'I thought I would call it THE SUDDENLY BOOK.'

'A very trenchant title,' said Larry. 'I feel, however, that your main characters could be padded out a little bit, in depth, as it were, before you get them all tangled up on the sofa.'

'Yes,' said Donald. 'You could well be right.'

'Well, that is interesting,' said Mother, sneezing violently. 'And now I think we really all ought to have a cup of tea.'

(Gerald Durrell, *Birds, Beasts and Relatives*)

hot foot: in a hurry
dehydrated: dried up
exasperated: irritated
gulped: swallowed noisily
trenchant: going straight to the point
padded out: presented in more detail
tangled up: mixed up

William McGonagall

[William McGonagall was a bad Scottish poet. In fact, his poetry was so bad that it became famous, and his books have sold far more copies than most collections of good poetry.]

A New Year's resolution to leave Dundee

Welcome! thrice welcome! to the year 1893,
For it is the year that I intend to leave Dundee,
Owing to the treatment I receive,
Which does my heart sadly grieve.
Every morning when I go out
The ignorant rabble they do shout
'There goes Mad McGonagall'
In derisive shouts, as loud as they can bawl,
And lifts stones and snowballs, throws them at me;
And such actions are shameful to be heard in the City of Dundee.
And I'm ashamed, kind Christians, to confess,
That from the Magistrates I can get no redress.
Therefore I have made up my mind, in the year of 1893
To leave the Ancient City of Dundee,
Because the citizens and me cannot agree.
The reason why? – because they disrespect me,
Which makes me feel rather discontent.
Therefore, to leave them I am bent;
And I will make my arrangements without delay,
And leave Dundee some early day.

William McGonagall

thrice: three times
grieve: distress, make unhappy
rabble: disorderly crowd
derisive: laughing unkindly
bawl: shout
redress: compensation
bent: determined

GCE (General Certificate of Education)

[English schoolchildren take two main exams: GCE O (ordinary) Level, at about 16, and GCE A (advanced) Level, at about 18. O Level is a general exam (but candidates can choose what subjects, and how many, they wish to attempt); for A Level, two or three subjects are studied in detail. Here is an extract from the regulations published by the Oxford Local Examinations Syndicate, one of the GCE examining bodies.]

ADVANCED LEVEL SYLLABUSES, 1977

ENGLISH LITERATURE

A 3

Three papers are set (3 hours each), Paper I being marked out of 104, Paper II out of 100, and Paper S out of 100. Papers I and II are the normal Advanced Level papers. Paper S is the Special Paper.

Paper I. Four books are set for detailed study. Candidates must answer questions on the Shakespeare play and on two of the other three books.

Paper II. Candidates must take one of the Papers A to F. Papers A to E are period papers and candidates are expected to show a general knowledge of the social and literary history of the period, with special reference to the works named. A passage for appreciation is set from each of two books marked with an asterisk. Candidates must attempt one of these. They must also answer three essay questions. Paper II F consists of questions on the content, form, and style of twelve books; candidates must answer three essay questions and a question testing appreciation of an unprepared passage, a choice of poetry and prose being given.

Paper S is set in such a way as to test whether candidates have studied the works prescribed for Papers I and II against the wider background of study normally explored in a sixth-form English Literature course. An optional appreciation question is included. No candidate is allowed to attempt more than three questions.

Paper I. Books for detailed study:

> **Either** Chaucer, *The Knight's Tale* (the whole of the Tale should be studied, but passages for translation and comment are set from Part II only). **Or** *Poetry of the Age of Chaucer* (Edward Arnold), ed. A. C. and J. E. Spearing: *The Friar's Tale, Sir Gawain and the Green Knight, Sir Orfeo* (passages for translation and comment are set only from *Sir Gawain and the Green Knight*)
> †Shakespeare, *Othello*
> †Milton, *Paradise Lost*, Book I
> Conrad, *Nostromo* (available in Penguin or Everyman or Pan)
>
> Extracts from Shakespeare are taken from *The Oxford Shakespeare* (*Oxford Standard Authors*, O.U.P.) edited by W. J. Craig, and extracts from Chaucer are taken from *The Works of Geoffrey Chaucer* (O.U.P.), edited by F. N. Robinson.

asterisk: mark like this: *
sixth-form: the top class in English schools
O.U.P.: Oxford University Press (a publishing house)

35

A Level answers

[Quotations from candidates' answers to questions in the GCE A Level English Literature examination.]

As for the plot of Othello, it hardly keep you on the edge of your seat.

Hamlet is the central character in this play as in many other plays by Shakespeare, notably Macbeth.

Shakespeare uses the ghost to attempt to hold the audience's attention.

Claudius has just married his late brother.

Ophelia strews flowers which is typical of Shakespeare's madness.

Chaucer has lasted for hundreds of years so he must have something in him.

Here Milton uses a lot of names which we do not understand without notes but this is always the case with Milton.

Tess had an illegible baby.

The word 'melt' is a very good adjective.

Life is a compound effigy of abstract theories.

keep(s) you on the edge of your seat: thrills you
strews: scatters
effigy: statue, sculpture

GCE O Level for idiots

Time allowed: three weeks.
Do not write on both sides of the paper at once.

1. Outline the most important features of astronomical theory under the later Babylonian empire OR Give the first name of Ringo Starr.
2. Would you ask William Shakespeare to   A. build a bridge   B. go sailing with you   C. lead an army   D. write a play?
3. What time is it when the big hand is on one and the little hand is on twelve?
4. How many commandments (approximately) was Moses given?
5. Spell 'psychoanalytically'.
6. Six kings of England have been called George, the last being George the sixth. Name the previous five.
7. Can you explain Einstein's special theory of relativity? (Answer yes or no.)

8. How long did the Seven Years' War last?
9. Which is the odd man out: *cat cat saxophone cat?*
10. Who wrote Beethoven's fifth symphony?

(Anonymous)

QUICK CROSSWORD

ACROSS

1 Bad (6)
4 Angry (5)
7 Secret (10)
8 Fall (4)
9 Rustic (5)
11 Beet variety (7)
13 Timely (7)
15 Explode (5)
17 Yearn (4)
18 Charge (10)
20 Number (5)
21 Decayed (6)

DOWN

1 Aimless (6)
2 Produce obtained (4)
3 Failure (7)
4 Drink (5)
5 Possess (3)
6 Time (5)
7 Secure control of (6)
10 Calculate (6)
12 Sceptic (7)
14 Pool (6)
15 Pair (5)
16 Restricted (5)
17 Mislaid (4)
19 Member (3)

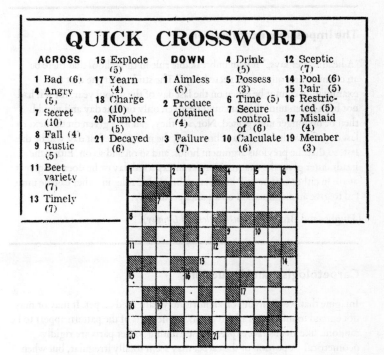

(*Daily Mail*)

[Solution on page 38.]

37

Solution to crossword on page 37

ACROSS : 1 Rancid. 4
Cross. 7 Confidence. 8 Drop. 9 Rural. 11 Mangold.
13 Topical. 15 Burst. 17 Long. 18 Allegation. 20
Eight. 21 Rotten. DOWN : 1 Random. 2 Crop. 3 Default.
4 Cider. 5 Own. 6 Spell. 7 Corner. 10 Reckon. 12
Doubter. 14 Lagoon. 15 Brace. 16 Tight. 17 Lost. 19
Leg.

The impossible examination

'A headmaster says, "It is an unbreakable rule in this school that there be
an examination on an unexpected day." The students argue that the
examination cannot be given on the last day of the school year, for if it had
not been given until then, it could be given only on that day and would
then be no longer unexpected. Nor, say they, can it be given on the next to
last day, for with the last day eliminated, the next to the last day will be the
last, so that the previous argument holds, and so on and so on. Either the
headmaster gives the examination on an expected day or he does not give it
at all. In either case he will break an unbreakable rule; in either case he must
fail to give an examination on an unexpected day.'

(Hughes and Brecht, *Vicious Circles and Infinity*)

Carpetologists and induction

Imagine that we are living on an intricately patterned carpet. It may or may
not extend to infinity in all directions. Some parts of the pattern appear to be
random, like an abstract expressionist painting; other parts are rigidly
geometrical. A portion of the carpet may seem totally irregular, but when
the same portion is viewed in a larger context, it becomes part of a subtle
symmetry.

The task of describing the pattern is made difficult by the fact that the
carpet is protected by a thick plastic sheet with a translucence that varies
from place to place. In certain places we can see through the sheet and
perceive the pattern; in others the sheet is opaque. The plastic sheet also
varies in hardness. Here and there we can scrape it down so that the pattern
is more clearly visible. In other places the sheet resists all efforts to make it
less opaque. Light passing through the sheet is often refracted in bizarre
ways, so that as more of the sheet is removed the pattern is radically
transformed. Everywhere there is a mysterious mixing of order and
disorder. Faint lattices with beautiful symmetries appear to cover the entire

rug, but how far they extend is anyone's guess. No one knows how thick the plastic sheet is. At no place has anyone scraped deep enough to reach the carpet's surface, if there is one.

Already the metaphor has been pushed too far. For one thing, the patterns of the real world, as distinct from this imaginary one, are constantly changing, like a carpet that is rolling up at one end while it is unrolling at the other end. Nevertheless, in a crude way the carpet can introduce some of the difficulties philosophers of science encounter in trying to understand why science works.

Induction is the procedure by which carpetologists, after examining parts of the carpet, try to guess what the unexamined parts look like. Suppose the carpet is covered with billions of tiny triangles. Whenever a blue triangle is found, it has a small red dot in one corner. After finding thousands of blue triangles, all with red dots, the carpetologists conjecture that all blue triangles have red dots. Each new blue triangle with a red dot is a confirming instance of the law. Provided that no counterexample is found, the more confirming instances there are, the stronger is the carpetologists' belief that the law is true.

(Martin Gardner, *Scientific American*)

intricately patterned: with a complicated pattern
random: unpredictable, irregular
subtle: complicated, difficult to analyse
symmetry: regularity
translucence: ability to let light pass through
is opaque: will not let light through
refracted: bent
bizarre: strange
radically: fundamentally
lattices: patterns of crossed lines
metaphor: image, comparison
crude: rough, inexact
conjecture: hypothesize, make a theory

A cartoon comment on inductive reasoning

Our planet's history

If you make a stack of newspapers day after day, at the end of the week Monday's paper will be at the bottom, and Sunday's at the top. Every newspaper is dated, but even if it were not, you could guess its date from its position in the pile. It is just like this with layers of sedimentary rock where the deepest layers are the oldest.

As each layer of sedimentary rock was formed, the plants and animals which were alive at that time became buried in it when they died. Usually they simply rotted away without any trace, but occasionally fossil skeletons have survived for millions of years. It is from these fossils that we learn about extinct plants, such as the giant tree ferns, and extinct animals, such as the great reptiles. It is rather like reading in one of the newspapers, picked out of our pile, about what happened on a particular day. We can tell from rocks that dinosaurs lived about two hundred million years ago, and early fishes five hundred million.

Fossils also give us clues about the climate when the fossilized organism was alive. For example, rocks in Greenland contain fossils of plants that can live only in a warm climate; so we can conclude that these northern regions must once have been warmer.

Fossils also give us other clues about changes to the Earth since they were laid down. Those of sea animals found in mountain ranges, for example, show that the areas which are mountains today were once probably under the sea. This evidence suggests that great earth movements must have taken place. Indeed, there is other evidence that on some occasions these movements were so violent that even the order of the rock layers was upset, just as if the order of our pile of papers had been upset. In the Grand Canyon of Arizona, the river has cut a gorge $1\frac{1}{2}$km deep so that the layers of rock (strata) built up over three hundred million years are clearly visible.

Rocks containing fossils help us to trace the Earth's history back six hundred million years. The older igneous rocks, which contain no fossils, cannot be used in this way, but scientists can calculate their age by testing the radioactive materials they contain: as radio-isotopes decay they form stable products. It is the ratio of active to stable material that provides an age clue from which it is estimated that the Earth started to cool about four thousand million years ago.

(*Penguin Book of the Physical World*)

sedimentary rock: rock formed from layers of earth, etc., deposited by running water

I like that stuff

Lovers lie around in it
Broken glass is found in it
Grass
I like that stuff

Tuna fish get trapped in it
Legs come wrapped in it
Nylon
I like that stuff

Eskimos and tramps chew it
Madame Tussaud gave status to it
Wax
I like that stuff

Elephants get sprayed with it
Scotch is made with it
Water
I like that stuff

Clergy are dumbfounded by it
Bones are surrounded by it
Flesh
I like that stuff

Harps are strung with it
Mattresses are sprung with it
Wire
I like that stuff

Carpenters make cots of it
Undertakers use lots of it
Wood
I like that stuff

Cigarettes are lit by it
Pensioners are happy when they sit by it
Fire
I like that stuff

Dankworth's alto is made of it, most of it,
Scoobedoo is composed of it
Plastic
I like that stuff

Man made fibres and raw materials
Old rolled gold and breakfast cereals
Platinum linoleum
I like that stuff

Skin on my hands
Hair on my head
Toenails on my feet
And linen on my bed

Well I like that stuff
Yes I like that stuff
The earth
Is made of earth
And I like that stuff

Adrian Mitchell

Madame Tussaud: the founder of a well-known museum in London which has wax
models of famous people
clergy: priests
dumbfounded: astonished, very surprised
undertakers: people who organize funerals
Dankworth: a jazz musician
alto: kind of saxophone
scoobedoo: ornamental work in plastic

Booming Dunes

A sand dune would not seem to be a very likely candidate as a natural sound generator. The fact is that dunes in many parts of the world squeak, roar or boom. Acoustic sands have been described in desert legend for at least 1,500 years, but they have received little scientific attention. Recently, however, David R. Criswell of the Lunar Science Institute in Houston, Tex., John F. Lindsay of the University of Texas at Galveston and David L. Reasoner of the Marshall Space Flight Center in Huntsville, Ala., conducted the first quantitative analysis of the properties of an acoustic dune.

The dune they investigated was Sand Mountain near Fallon, Nev., which has often been heard to boom. In order to obtain simultaneous recordings of both seismic and acoustic emissions from the sand, the experimenters and two assistants set up a geophone for monitoring vibrations transmitted through the sand and a microphone for receiving sounds transmitted through the air. After trying several different methods they found that the sand boomed loudest when a trench was rapidly dug in it with a flat-bladed shovel. The sound was like a short, low note on a cello; it lasted for less than two seconds and was readily audible at a distance of 30 meters. The booming could also be produced by pulling the sand downhill with the hand; in that case strong vibrations reminiscent of a mild electric shock could be felt in the fingertips.

Although the appearance of booming sand dunes is indistinguishable from that of ordinary silent dunes, examination of sands in the scanning electron microscope revealed that the individual grains of booming sand are more highly polished than the grains of silent sand. Twenty-nine of the 31 known booming dunes are composed primarily of quartz sand; the exceptions are two dunes in Hawaii that are principally

43

calcite sand.

The tonal quality of the booming is remarkably pure, comparable to an organ tone. "One must be amazed that as unlikely a medium as sand can produce such pure oscillations," the experimenters comment in *Journal of Geophysical Research*. "A quantitative theory of the booming process is not presently available.... The problem is intriguing and very likely far more complicated physically and mathematically than the simple processes controlling oscillations in an organ pipe."

(*Scientific American*)

Sounds unfriendly

Noise annoys. It affects individuals physically and psychologically. Two recent studies by psychologists Kenneth Mathews and Lance Canon now suggest that noise can also influence how nice we are to others.

Mathews and Canon set up an experiment to see how noise would affect people in an everyday setting that gave them a chance to help another man in trouble. As a potential subject walked past a suburban semi-detached, he saw a man (one of the experimenters) carrying two boxes overflowing with books from a car to the house. As the passer-by came closer, the book carrier dropped several books and, as he tried to save them, he spilled more onto the pavement. The other researcher, hiding on the other side of the road, observed whether the passer-by offered to help.

When the noise level of the street was normal (about 50 decibels), 20 percent of the passers-by stopped to help. To make his need more dramatic, the experimenter sometimes wore a cast on his arm. When he did, 80 percent of the subjects offered to help.

But when a motor lawnmower was turned on in a nearby garden, good Samaritanism turned sour. With the noise level at 87 decibels only 10 percent of the passers-by helped the unhandicapped man, and only 15 percent came to the aid of the man with a cast.

The simplest explanation seemed to be that people were less helpful when it was noisy because they wanted to escape the noise as soon as they could. So Mathews and Canon set up a similar experiment in a situation where the subjects couldn't get away.

This time a student volunteer waited in a room before being called for the experiment he expected. The experimenter waited in the same room with a pile of books on his lap. When his name was called he got up, dropping his books in the process. Again the experimenters varied the room noise level from normal (48 dB) to loud (85 dB). Again, like the passers-by in the street, nearly three-quarters of the 52 students helped pick up the books under normal conditions, but only half that many volunteered when the room was noisy.

This time the subjects' behaviour could not be explained by an urge to escape the noise. Helping the book fumbler would not lengthen the time spent in the noisy waiting room. In fact, helping could even shorten the time if each man presumed he was next in line after the fumbler finished his turn.

Mathews and Canon suggest two explanations. Perhaps noise is distracting, so the men didn't notice and respond as quickly to the book-dropping incident under noisy conditions. Or perhaps the book-dropping further annoyed students already irritated by the noise, making them less likely to help out. Either way, it seems that Good Samaritanism is a lot more complicated than it seemed on the road from Jerusalem to Jericho.

(*Psychology Today*)

setting: situation
potential subject: person who might be used in the experiment
semi-detached: semi-detached house (one divided down the middle into homes for two separate families)
decibels: units for measuring noise
cast: plaster covering worn on a broken arm or leg
good Samaritanism: reference to the story in the Bible about a Samaritan (member of a particular Jewish tribe) who helped a man in trouble on the road from Jerusalem to Jericho, after other people had passed by without stopping
fumbler: fumbling is handling things clumsily

Pollution

Pollution, pollution – you can use the latest toothpaste
And then rinse your mouth with industrial waste

Just go out for a breath of air
And you'll be ready for medicare.
The city streets are quite a thrill –
If the hoods don't get you the monoxide will.

Pollution, pollution – wear a gas mask and a veil,
Then you can breathe – long as you don't inhale.

Fish gotta swim, birds gotta fly –
But they don't last long if they try.

Tom Lehrer

medicare: free medical treatment provided by the state in USA
hoods: (slang) gangsters
monoxide: carbon monoxide – one of the gases given out by car engines
gotta: (spoken American) have got to

A fable for tomorrow

[This text is taken from the introduction to Rachel Carson's book *Silent Spring*, whose publication in 1962 made people aware, for the first time, of the dangers of pollution by insecticides and chemical fertilizers.]

There was once a town in the heart of America where all life seemed to live in harmony with its surroundings. The town lay in the midst of a checkerboard of prosperous farms, with fields of grain and hillsides of orchards where, in spring, white clouds of bloom drifted above the green fields. In autumn, oak and maple and birch set up a blaze of colour that flamed and flickered across a backdrop of pines. Then foxes barked in the hills and deer silently crossed the fields, half hidden in the mists of the autumn mornings.

Along the roads, laurel, viburnum and alder, great ferns and wildflowers, delighted the traveller's eye through much of the year. Even in winter the roadsides were places of beauty, where countless birds came to feed on the berries and on the seed heads of the dried weeds rising above the snow. The countryside was, in fact, famous for the abundance and variety of its bird life, and when the flood of migrants was pouring through in spring and autumn people travelled from great distances to observe them. Others came to fish the streams, which flowed clear and cold out of the hills and contained shady pools where trout lay. So it had been from the days many years ago when the first settlers raised their houses, sank their wells, and built their barns.

Then a strange blight crept over the area and everything began to change. Some evil spell had settled on the community: mysterious maladies swept the flocks of chickens; the cattle and sheep sickened and died. Everywhere was a shadow of death. The farmers spoke of much illness among their families. In the town the doctors had become more and more puzzled by new kinds of sickness appearing among their patients. There had been several sudden and unexplained deaths, not only among adults but even among children, who would be stricken suddenly while at play and die within a few hours.

There was a strange stillness. The birds, for example – where had they gone? Many people spoke of them, puzzled and disturbed. The feeding stations in the backyards were deserted. The few birds seen anywhere were moribund; they trembled violently and could not fly. It was a spring without voices. On the mornings that had once throbbed with the dawn chorus of robins, catbirds, doves, jays, wrens, and scores of other bird voices there was now no sound; only silence lay over the fields and woods and marsh.

On the farms the hens brooded, but no chicks were hatched. The farmers complained that they were unable to raise any pigs – the litters were small and the young survived only a few days. The apple trees were coming into bloom but no bees droned among the blossoms, so there was no pollination and there would be no fruit.

The roadsides, once so attractive, were now lined with browned and withered vegetation as though swept by fire. These too, were silent, deserted by all living things. Even the streams were now lifeless. Anglers no longer visited them, for all the fish had died.

In the gutters under the eaves and between the shingles of the roofs, a white granular powder still showed a few patches; some weeks before it had fallen like snow upon the roofs and the lawns, the fields and streams.

No witchcraft, no enemy action had silenced the rebirth of new life in this stricken world. The people had done it themselves.

This town does not actually exist, but it might easily have a thousand counterparts in America or elsewhere in the world. I know of no community that has experienced all the misfortunes I describe. Yet every one of these disasters has actually happened somewhere, and many real communities

47

have already suffered a substantial number of them. A grim spectre has crept upon us almost unnoticed, and this imagined tragedy may easily become a stark reality we all shall know.

(Rachel Carson, *Silent Spring*)

checkerboard: pattern of light and dark squares
bloom: blossom (the flowers on trees)
backdrop: scenery in the background
migrants: birds that fly to warm countries in the winter
blight: plant disease
spell: state resulting from the use of magic
maladies: illnesses
stricken: struck down
feeding stations: tables for birds to feed at
backyards: open spaces behind houses
moribund: dying
throbbed: vibrated
brooded: sat on their eggs
pollination: fertilization of plants
gutters: channels to carry rainwater away
eaves: edges of the roofs
shingles: wooden roof tiles
witchcraft: magic activity of witches
spectre: frightening supernatural power
stark: tragic

How birds fly

Birds are adapted for flying in several ways. Their forelimbs are specialized as wings covered with flight feathers; they have powerful wing muscles, a rigid body skeleton, light hollow bones, a large heart and well-developed nervous system. There is also a system of air sacs within the bones and between the body organs which provides extra air for the increased respiration while the bird is in flight.

The wings are concave below and convex above and have a thick front (leading) edge tapering off to a thin (trailing) edge, like the wings of an aeroplane. They provide the initial lift to launch the bird in the air, and then give it forward propulsion through the air. Birds take off with a jump or short run, preferably into the wind, followed by a powerful semicircular beating of wings which produces lift on the downstroke and forward thrust on the upstroke. After gaining height the wings move with an up-and-down flapping, with the lift and thrust coming from the downbeat. The tail helps to steer and the legs are tucked out of the way so that the body is smooth and streamlined.

Waterfowl, such as ducks and swans, have greater difficulty in taking off straight from the water without a firm surface to push

Birds in flight. The diagram shows movements of a duck's wings.

from. To overcome this they raise themselves with much more wing flapping. When landing, a bird slows down by widening its wings and tail and pushing its body vertically downwards to act as an air brake. A moulting bird which has lost its tail feathers lands badly because it cannot slow down quickly enough. Some birds can fly far and fast. Reliable figures are difficult to obtain, but ducks are said to fly at up to 100 kph and swifts even faster, while the peregrine falcon is said to dive at 150 kph or more. In general, the faster birds have longer and narrower wings. All birds flap their wings when they fly. A hummingbird flaps at up to 60 beats a second, but some birds save their energy by soaring and gliding. Gliding birds such as gulls and albatrosses climb or soar then gradually lose height. Vultures and some eagles soar well, using rising currents of warm air like glider pilots. Gliding birds have long narrow wings, while soarers have long broad ones.

Man's attempts to fly by imitating birds have failed, often fatally. He would need a much bigger heart, and flapping muscles that made up half his body weight, to fly in this manner.

(*The Penguin Book of the Natural World*)

forelimbs: front limbs
respiration: breathing
concave: with a hollow curve
convex: the opposite of concave – with a bulging curve
tapering: getting thinner
launch: push off
thrust: push
tucked: folded
streamlined: designed to offer little resistance to the air
moulting: losing its feathers
soaring: riding on rising air currents
gliding: drifting downwards through the air without making any effort

49

Jonathan Livingston Seagull

Most gulls don't bother to learn more than the simplest facts of flight – how to get from shore to food and back again. For most gulls, it is not flying that matters, but eating. For this gull, though, it was not eating that mattered, but flight. More than anything else, Jonathan Livingston Seagull loved to fly.

This kind of thinking, he found, is not the way to make one's self popular with other birds. Even his parents were dismayed as Jonathan spent whole days alone, making hundreds of low-level glides, experimenting.

He didn't know why, for instance, but when he flew at altitudes less than half his wingspan above the water, he could stay in the air longer, with less effort. His glides ended not with the usual feet-down splash into the sea, but with a long flat wake as he touched the surface with his feet tightly stream-lined against his body. When he began sliding in to feet-up landings on the beach, then pacing the length of his slide in the sand, his parents were very much dismayed indeed.

'Why, Jon, *why*?' his mother asked. 'Why is it so hard to be like the rest of the flock, Jon? Why can't you leave low flying to the pelicans, the albatross? Why don't you *eat*? Jon, you're bone and feathers!'

'I don't mind being bone and feathers, Mum. I just want to know what I can do in the air and what I can't, that's all. I just want to know.'

'See here, Jonathan,' said his father, not unkindly. 'Winter isn't far away. Boats will be few, and the surface fish will be swimming deep. If you must study, then study food, and how to get it. This flying business is all very well, but you can't eat a glide, you know. Don't you forget that the reason you fly is to eat.'

Jonathan nodded obediently. For the next few days he tried to behave like the other gulls; he really tried, screeching and fighting with the flock around the piers and fishing boats, diving on scraps of fish and bread. But he couldn't make it work.

It's all so pointless, he thought, deliberately dropping a hard-won anchovy to a hungry old gull chasing him. I could be spending all this time learning to fly. There's so much to learn!

It wasn't long before Jonathan Gull was off by himself again, far out at sea, hungry, happy, learning.

The subject was speed, and in a week's practice he learned more about speed than the fastest gull alive.

From a thousand feet, flapping his wings as hard as he could, he pushed over into a blazing steep dive toward the waves, and learned why seagulls don't make blazing steep power-dives. In just six seconds he was moving seventy miles per hour, the speed at which one's wing goes unstable on the upstroke.

Time after time it happened. Careful as he was, working at the very peak of his ability, he lost control at high speed.

Climb to a thousand feet. Full power straight ahead first, then push over, flapping, to a vertical dive. Then, every time, his left wing stalled on an upstroke, he'd roll violently left, stall his right wing recovering, and flick like fire into a wild tumbling spin to the right.

He couldn't be careful enough on that upstroke. Ten times he tried, and all ten times, as he passed through seventy miles per hour, he burst into a churning mass of feathers, out of control, crashing down into the water.

The key, he thought at last, dripping wet, must be to hold the wings still at high speeds – to flap up to fifty and then hold the wings still.

From two thousand feet he tried again, rolling into his dive, beak straight down, wings full out and stable from the moment he passed fifty miles per hour. It took tremendous strength, but it worked. In ten seconds he had blurred through ninety miles per hour. Jonathan had set a world speed record for seagulls!

(Richard Bach, *Jonathan Livingston Seagull*)

gulls: various kinds of large seabird
wingspan: length from wingtip to wingtip
wake: track made by something moving through water
pier: platform built out over the sea for unloading boats
scraps: small pieces
unstable: unsteady, not controlled
stalled: stuck, refused to move
churning: turning violently
blurred: the word suggests a movement so fast it cannot be seen

"Excuse me, but would you mind scratching my nose?"

(*Punch*)

Note to the hurrying man

All day I sit here doing nothing but
watching how at daybreak
birds fly out and return no fatter
when it's over. Yet hurrying about this room
you would have me do something similar;
would have me make myself a place
in that sad traffic you call a world.

Don't hurry me into it;
no excuses, no apologies.
Until their brains snap open
I have no love for those who rush
about its mad business;
put their children on a starting line and push
into Christ knows what madness.

You will not listen.
'Work at life!' you scream.
and working I see you rushing everywhere,
so fast most times you ignore
two quarters of your half a world.

If all slow things are useless
and take no active part in nor justify your ignorance
that's fine; but why bother screaming after me?
Afraid perhaps to come to where I've stopped
in case you find
into some slow and glowing countryside
yourself escaping.
Screams measure and keep up the distance between us:

Be quieter –
I really do need to escape;
take the route you might take
if ever this hurrying is over.

Brian Patten

daybreak: dawn, sunrise
snap open: open suddenly (with sudden understanding)

It was a slow day for news until this pink pig took wing

By Clive Borrell

It was a slow news day so I telephoned the Yard. "Sorry, there is very little crime about".

I grunted and wondered whether to write out my expenses. "I can offer you a flying pink pig if you like."

I grunted again. "I see those every morning", I said.

"Really. There's a flying pink pig loose at 7,000 feet and it's causing a hazard to aircraft."

I told him to look at his calendar. "There are months to go before April 1", I said.

I told the news editor there was no crime about. "You can have a flying pink pig if you fancy it", I offered. "Get some more coffee. It might help", he advised.

Twenty minutes later I decided to ring someone else at the Yard. "Not much about I'm afraid unless you're interested in a flying pink pig", he said, and laughed.

"Do you want me to tell you about it?" I knew I was not going to get any peace until he did.

"At 10.25 this morning a pink pig balloon measuring 10 metres by five metres, escaped from its mooring in the car park of Battersea power station. It was there to advertise the pop group, Pink Floyd, but it broke loose.

"One of our helicopters on traffic patrol intercepted a radio message from a light aircraft to the control tower at Heathrow airport. The pilot was heard to say: "I've just been overtaken by a pink elephant at 7,000 feet.

"The helicopter crew offered to help because the control tower could not plot the creature on their radar."

He paused. "Don't tell me—you chased it", I said in disbelief. "No, we escorted it across London as far as Crystal Palace. Now it's out of our area", he said regretfully.

At noon the helium balloon was 20 miles east of London over the Essex suburbs and the Civil Aviation Authority was also infected by mirth.

"It's the best laugh we've had for ages. We've told all aircraft to keep an eye out for it. You can imagine the shock some passengers would get if a pig flew past."

Later police in Essex reported: "It's at about 5,000 feet and seems to be coming down. It must be getting hungry." I groaned. I gave up grunting when I realized the significance of the noise.

By mid-afternoon the pig was 18,000 feet above Chatham, and gave every appearance of heading home to Germany, where it was made.

But several hours later it became deflated and subsided disconsolately on to a farm at Chilham, near Canterbury.

(*The Times*)

---

the Yard: Scotland Yard (London detective headquarters)   grunted: made a low noise (like a pig)   hazard: danger   mooring: place where it was tied up
plot: find the position of   helium: a gas   mirth: laughter
became deflated: lost its gas   subsided: came down   disconsolately: unhappily

53

As I sat under the apple tree
A birdie sent his love to me,
And as I wiped it from my eye
I said 'Thank goodness cows can't fly'.

(Children's rhyme)

The projectionist's nightmare

This is the projectionist's nightmare:
A bird finds its way into the cinema,
finds the beam, flies down it,
smashes into a screen depicting a garden,
a sunset and two people being nice to each other.
Real blood, real intestines, slither down
the likeness of a tree.
'This is no good,' screams the audience,
'This is not what we came to see.'

Brian Patten

projectionist: person who handles the machinery in a cinema
intestines: digestive tubes
slither: slide

Cinema in a heatwave

USELESS to pretend that cinema-going last week was anything but a pain in the neck, and a sweat in most other parts. It was hot in London. You could drink a bar of chocolate and draw your pop-corn from its bag in one great encrusted lump, like a geological sample. Air-reconditioned for the umpteenth time (no longer air at all, but Breathe-o-tex), came and lapped round you, as if asking to be let out. But at least the films were short.

(From a film review by Russell Davies in *The Observer*)

a pain in the neck: (slang) boring, a nuisance
pop-corn: kind of sweet made from dried maize
umpteenth: umpteen is a slang word meaning a large number
to lap: the movement of little waves

Film Index

ALL THE PRESIDENT'S MEN. Cert. AA. Alan J. Pakula's definitive film on Watergate. A very precise and important film. Dustin Hoffman, Robert Redford, Jason Robards. 138 mins. **Scene One** and **Warner West End One.**

BARRY LYNDON. Cert. A. Stanley Kubrick's vastly underrated adaptation of Thackeray's novel, with a keen insight into the mood of the times. All about the ambitions of an Irish rogue. Ryan O'Neal, Marisa Berenson. 187 mins. **Warner West End Three.**

BED HOSTESSES. Cert. X. Sex comedy? The worst of the worst. Marianne Dupont, Martina Domingo. Swiss. 63 mins. **Jacey, Leicester Square.**

THE BEST OF THE NEW YORK EROTIC FILM FESTIVAL. Cert. X (London). In fact the best of two such Festivals, of 1972 & 3: a collection of crude sex cartoons, erotic and in one case actually artistic shorts. 75 mins. **Pigalle Cinema.**

THE BINGO LONG TRAVELLING ALL-STARS AND MOTOR KINGS. Cert. A. Financially successful American comedy on baseball, featuring an all-black cast. James Earl Jones, Billie Dee Williams, Richard Pryor. 111 mins. **Plaza One** (from Oct. 28).

BLACK EMANUELLE. Cert. X. Italian sex drama with Emanuelle and Karin Schubert. No more original than its title. 96 mins. **Centa Cinema.**

BREAKING POINT. Cert. X. Crime thriller with Robert Culp, Bo Svenson and Belinda J. Montgomery. 92 mins. **Studio Two** (until Oct. 23).

BUGSY MALONE. Cert. U. Musical which takes the old gangster formula of the 20-30's, laughs wittily at the clichés, adds a series of modern musical numbers and turns over the whole thing to a cast of children to interpret. 93 mins. **Odeon Marble Arch.**

X Film passed as suitable for exhibition to adults only, no one under 18 will be admitted.

AA Passed as suitable for exhibition to persons of 14 years and over, no one under the age of 14 will be admitted.

A Passed for general exhibition, but parents and guardians are warned that the film may include material not suitable for persons under 14 to see.

U Passed for general exhibition.

(*What's On in London*)

underrated: undervalued (better than people realize)
crude: with no artistic value
clichés: expressions or ideas that have been used so often that they are no longer interesting

55

The Six Million Dollar Man's sex life

[The Six Million Dollar Man is a character in a television series who has had parts of his body replaced, after an accident, by electronically controlled machinery.]

THE Six Million Dollar Man (Thames) has acquired a steady girlfriend, called Bionic Woman. Since either of them, in a careless moment, would be capable of pushing over a building with one hand, the question arises of how they manage their love life.

Although a fairly steady follower of Six's adventures, I long ago forgot which bits of him have been replaced with high-performance hardware. The eyes and legs for certain, and at least one arm. It would be indelicate to speculate whether the more intimate sections of his bodily fabric are similarly crammed with transistors and solenoids. The same inhibition applies to discussing some of the attributes of Bionic Woman. But even granting that the two lovers remain organic in those areas, they would still surely be capable of doing each other fearful damage in the spasms of rapture. Six can carve a doorway through a brick wall with his index finger. Imagine what he could do with a single misplaced caress. He could break every circuit in her body. They'd be lying there in a heap of wires and a puddle of hydraulic fluid.

(From a television review by Clive James in *The Observer*)

indelicate: rude, tactless
transistors and solenoids: electronic devices
inhibition: taboo
attributes: features, characteristics
organic: natural, made of flesh and blood
spasms of rapture: violent movements of passion
hydraulic fluid: liquid used for transmitting pressure (e.g. in the braking system of a car)

An American women's group is asking a toy firm to stop advertising a doll that grows breasts when its arm is twisted. 'It is a gross caricature of the female body that invites ridicule' and it 'caters to psychotic pre-occupation with the instant sex object,' the group says.

(*Psychology Today*)

caters to: appeals to

Sex education in schools

[This is a transcription of part of a tape-recorded conversation between two people (A and B). The text is specially marked so as to show those elements of spoken language which are usually lost when a conversation is written down – intonation, stress and rhythm, noises of hesitation and agreement, etc. The meaning of the signs is as follows:

| : boundary between tone-units
| : first stressed syllable in a tone-unit
` ´ – ^ ˅ : falling, rising, level, rising–falling, and falling–rising tones
ˡ : stressed syllable
ˡˡ : syllable with extra strong stress
↑ : stressed, high-pitched syllable
. – – –: pauses of different lengths
Capital letters : words with strongest stress in a tone-unit.]

B but er · |you're 'teaching – erm at a GRÀMMAR school| |ÀREN'T you|

A |YÈS| · |YÈS|

B   well |what do you 'think about ↑SÈX edu'cation| – do you |think that er i it er I |mean · there's |been a a a 'great ↑ˡˡHÒOha about it| (|M̌|) |RÈCENTLY| |HÀSN'T there| and erm – er about a |FÌLM that was 'made| and |só on| (M|HḾ|) – – well what |what are YÒUR 'views on it| – –

A |I find that – – 'with so ↑MÂNY of these 'problems| · |MÀRRIAGE| |SÈX edu'cation| · as |soon as you 'try and 'make it · a sort of ↑formal ↑LÈSSON| – – the |whole 'thing 'falls FLÀT| – –

B |M̌|

A you |KNÓW| |if you used to have a – – ↑period · |we used to 'have one 'called DISCÙSSION 'groups| – – and you were |LÀNDED with| – – m |TWÈLVE| |SÌXTEEN| · |BÒYS| – |ˡˡin a RÒOM| · and |there you WÈRE| you were sup|posed to DISCÙSS| – |could be ÀNYTHING| – – but · |it was so ↑DÌFFICULT| it was |so ARTI↑FÌCIAL| ·

B |M̌|

A whereas · |teaching 'something like ↑ÈNGLISH of 'course| – a |LÒT of 'these SÚBJECTS| |come up ↑fairly ↑NÀTURALLY| – |and you can DIS↑CÙSS them| · |in the ↑CÔNTEXT of the 'class| |ˡˡWHÈN they ARÍSE| – and |ˡˡǓSUALLY 'then it be'comes| – |much 'more 'SATIS↑FÀCTORY| – – |and you get ↑LÒTS of 'questions|

B   I I · I |quite A↑GRÈE with 'that|
(|YÈS|) I mean it's a it's a it's a |WÌDE| sort of · |open
↑ÈNDED| |SÙBJECT ÉNGLISH| (|YÈS|) |ÌSN'T it| (|YÈS|) but the
|trouble is it ↑does de'pend on the ↑TÈACHER| because there
|are 'some 'teachers (|oh EN↑TÌRELY|) who ↑just – ↑WÒN'T| I
|mean as ↑far (|M̀|) as THÈY'RE CONCÉRNED| they they're |doing
a TÈXT| you |KNÓW| I |mean they're · they may be |reading
'something by ↑SHĂKESPEARE| (|M̀|) and |that's ↑ÌT| I er there's
|no ↑QUÈSTION |of EX"TÈNDING it in 'any 'way| (|NÒ|) and
|"ĂLSO| they |have their ↑own in ↑INHI↑BÌTIONS about 'talking
about 'sex| (of |CÒURSE|) I |mean they're ↑just not ↑FRÀNK
a'bout it|

(Crystal and Davy, *Advanced Conversational English*)

a great hooha: exaggerated public discussion
falls flat: fails to interest people
period: class, lesson
you were landed with: (slang) you found yourself having to look after
open-ended subject: subject that can lead in many different directions
frank: open, honest

A sex education lesson

Miss Wilkins, Chemistry teacher:
    'As you know, children, this school – much against my will – has decided
to commence a course in "sex" education. I have (unfortunately) been
chosen to attempt to undertake the first lesson. The headmaster (as some of
you girls may know) is very interested in . . . in . . . this aspect of education.
He has decided that we should teach . . . "sex" in complete frankness.
    '. . . girls . . . girls and . . . and boys well, are . . . are . . . well . . .
slightly different. Boys . . . boys have . . . something that girls have not.
This is called a . . . well, you know a . . . "tinkle" – which you know all
about, don't you Johnny? Stop that Johnny! leave it alone! – No, Jimmy,
you may not give us a demonstration. Did you hear that Jimmy! Jimmy!
Pull your trousers up immediately!
    'Girls . . . or . . . you may have noticed a lack . . . a loss . . . a slight
deficiency in that part of your anatomy. Instead of . . . of . . . of having . . .
having what boys have, you have a "babyhole". . . .
    'Yes Johnny, I know you want to know how babies are born. I'm coming
to that – No Mark, I will not give a demonstration! And that goes for you
too Johnny! Johnny leave Susan alone!

'Now before I start, I want to make it absolutely clear that I personally think that the whole thing is disgusting. I have never attempted – and will never attempt – this ugly procedure. I think nature could have quite easily have found a much "naicer" way of achieving the same result! But if you insist on propagating yourselves, which I don't doubt for an instant, this is the method you shall be forced to adopt. . . .

'I now have some diagrams to show you, which frankly are a complete revelation to me. I already knew it was pretty disgusting, but I certainly wasn't prepared for such filth! Yes, Jimmy, I know you don't agree! And you too Mark! . . .'

Madeleine Rilla, 14

(Quoted in Nan Berger, *Rights*)

tinkle: (slang) small children's word for penis
"naicer": affected pronunciation of nicer
propagating yourselves: having children
filth: emphatic word for dirt

"WE HAD SEX TODAY"

(*Private Eye*)

Teenagers and sex

[Extracts from interviews with British schoolchildren.]

'I think if you asked all the sixth-formers in this school, they'd nearly all say they'd like to be virgins when they get married. I wouldn't like to make love to my boyfriend, not when I'm so young.' *(Susan, 17)*

'I don't think it's vital to keep your virginity until you get married, but I shall myself. It's up to the individual. When I say I'm proud to be a virgin, people laugh. I don't think it's funny – I *am* proud of it. . . . Girls seem to be less open about sex than boys. I don't think it's wrong to talk about it, but it's the sort of thing I prefer to keep to myself. Girls talk about sex when they're in a bunch of girls, but not much with boys because it's embarrassing.' *(Lindsay, 15)*

'Well, *I* made love to the boy I was engaged to last year. It comes naturally, you know. I did it because I wanted to know what it was like and I knew it would please him. I was happy because I knew *he* was happy. But I couldn't do it with anybody else – it's got to be an important relationship.' *(Julie, 16)*

'I started going out with girls when I was 12. I have a girlfriend I like very much, but we don't make love. I don't think premarital sex is a good thing. People keep getting disappointed and trying new partners, trying to find the right one. I think it's better to get married and settle down first.' *(Ken, 15)*

'I started going out with girls when I was 13. I only make love to a girl if we really both want to. Sex isn't just a physical sensation; it depends on interest and understanding. The only time I made love to a girl just because she attracted me physically, it was a bit of an anticlimax afterwards because we couldn't talk. The whole essence of sex is communication. I remember the first time I had sex, it wasn't very good, and I couldn't talk about it to the girl or discuss it with my parents. That was really upsetting.' *(Richard, 17)*

'I started having sex 6 months ago. Sure I enjoy it, otherwise I wouldn't do it. It's the older generation who degrade sex, really. Parents are so bloody-minded, telling you it's wrong all the time, they just encourage you to experiment, like with drugs or drinking. I hope I'll be a better parent than my father in that respect, but I know it's difficult. There should be more sex education in schools – in my girlfriend's school, they're doing sex as a social studies project – I think that's a good thing.' *(Daniel, 16)*

premarital: before marriage
degrade sex: reduce its value
bloody-minded: (slang) deliberately annoying

I'm still a virgin . . .

Dear Jill,
My problem is that I have never been out
with a boy or had sexual intercourse. I am
still a virgin and I am 16.
Is there something wrong with me?

Certainly not! It may seem that everybody is
rushing round going out with half a dozen different boys and sleeping with people all over the
place, but it's a myth you know. There are plenty
of girls and boys who have never been on a date
or even if they have, they have probably not had
sex with someone. They may boast that they
have because they've got this daft idea that it
makes them look bigger. So I wouldn't worry if I
were you. Get out and about and meet boys, by
all means, but don't think you've got to fall in
love with any of them or go to bed with them.
Enjoy yourself and stop worrying.

(*O.K.* magazine)

SIR – I read with interest your report (October
9) that it is not a sexual offence for a woman
to have sex with a boy. It is, of course, a sexual
offence for a *man* to have sex with a boy.

On the other hand, whereas it is a sexual
offence for a woman to importune a man, it
is not an offence for a man to importune a
woman.

So if Mr X importunes Mrs Y while she
is having sex with Master Z, this is apparently
fine, but if Mrs Y importunes Mr X while *he*
is having sex with Master Z, they have all
had it.

Is this not a most peculiar kind of sexual
discrimination? – Yours faithfully,

BRIAN SIMPSON.
161 Gloucester Place
London NW1.

(*Guardian*)

importune: invite for sexual purposes (used for prostitutes)
Master: title used instead of *Mr* for boys
they have all had it: they are all in trouble

Judge says sex ban legislation is 'baffling'

After being told at the Central Criminal Court yesterday that a man of 22 had had sexual intercourse with a girl, aged 15 from a boarding school in Surrey with her consent, Judge McKinnon, QC, said : " Sshe has no complaints at all ; a thoroughly satisfactory experience so far as she is concerned."

Jonathan Groves, a carpenter, of Bell Crescent, Horley, Surrey, pleaded guilty to having unlawful sexual intercourse with the girl earlier this year.

Judge McKinnon said : " The trouble is, this law stands as an attempt to protect fully mature young women against their own natural inclinations. But how on earth an ysociety can delude itself into thinking that that sort of law can have any sort of success baffles me."

He continued : " I have no doubt that she was a perfectly good girl, and there does not seem to be a record of promiscuity in connexion with offences of this sort concerning the denefdant.

" How do you vindicate a law of this character which is so controversial ? When you have got young women of this age and this maturity participating in a perfectly natural activity, it is difficult to brand the other partner as a criminal."

Conditionally discharging Mr Groves for 12 months, the judge said : " Be careful in your choice of girl friends in future because you might have some other judge who takes a more serious view."

(*The Times*)

ban: prohibition, law against
consent: agreement
baffles me: I can't understand it
promiscuity: having sex with lots of different people
vindicate: justify
controversial: the subject of disagreement
brand: name, label (with a bad name)
conditionally discharging: releasing him without punishment, on condition that he kept out of trouble

---

Small children's ideas about love

I know what love is, its the stuff they sell on the telly.

Clara aged 4

My mummy says my Daddy is in love with his car and when I grow up I shall have two.

Roger aged 6

kittens

My cat falls in love and stays out all night and then he brings a lot of kittens back.

Henry aged 6

my aunty falls in love
when we go on holiday but
She never likes it and
She cries

Leonard aged 6

I once saw some one fall in love
In a car. It wasn't going though.

Sally aged 7

(Collected by Nanette Newman)

telly: (slang) television

A Proposale

[This is an extract from the famous story 'The Young Visiters', written by a nine-year-old girl. It was published exactly as she wrote it, with spelling and punctuation unchanged.]

Let us now bask under the spreading trees said Bernard in a passiunate tone.

Oh yes lets said Ethel and she opened her dainty parasole and sank down upon the long green grass. She closed her eyes but she was far from asleep. Bernard sat beside her in profound silence gazing at her pink face and long wavy eye lashes. He puffed at his pipe for some moments while the larks gaily caroled in the blue sky. Then he edged a trifle closer to Ethels form.

Ethel he murmered in a trembly voice.

Oh what is it said Ethel hastily sitting up.

Words fail me ejaculated Bernard horsly my passion for you is intense he added fervently. It has grown day and night since I first beheld you.

Oh said Ethel in susprise I am not prepared for this and she lent back against the trunk of the tree.

Bernard placed one arm tightly round her. When will you marry me Ethel he uttered you must be my wife it has come to that I love you so intensly that if you say no I shall perforce dash my body to the brink of yon muddy river he panted wildly.

64

Oh dont do that implored Ethel breathing rarther hard.

Then say you love me he cried.

Oh Bernard she sighed fervently I certainly love you madly you are to me like a Heathen god she cried looking at his manly form and handsome flashing face I will indeed marry you.

How soon gasped Bernard gazing at her intensly.

As soon as possible said Ethel gently closing her eyes.

My Darling whispered Bernard and he seiezed her in his arms we will be married next week.

Oh Bernard muttered Ethel this is so sudden.

No no cried Bernard and taking the bull by both horns he kissed her violently on her dainty face. My bride to be he murmered several times.

Ethel trembled with joy as she heard the mistick words.

Oh Bernard she said little did I ever dream of such as this and she suddenly fainted into his out stretched arms.

proposale: (correct spelling *proposal*) offer of marriage
bask: sunbathe
parasole: (correct spelling *parasol*) sunshade
caroled: (correct spelling *carolled*) sang
ejaculated: exclaimed suddenly
horsly: (correct spelling *hoarsely*) in a voice rough with emotion
fervently: passionately
beheld: saw
uttered: said
perforce: be forced to
brink: edge
yon: that
panted: said breathlessly
implored: begged
heathen: non–Christian
taking the bull by both horns: (normally *by the horns*) acting decisively
bride to be: future wife

Small children's ideas about marriage

I've been marrid five times, mostly with my mother, but once I did get marrid to a girl who gave me some chewing gum, But that was on holiday.

Leslie aged 7

65

I would like to marry my dog.
but it isint alowed, is it?

Bruce aged 6

I think you can fall in love if you have your picture taken in frunt of the church.

Eric aged 5

(Collected by Nanette Newman)

somewhere i have never travelled

somewhere i have never travelled, gladly beyond
any experience, your eyes have their silence:
in your most frail gesture are things which enclose me
or which i cannot touch because they are too near.

your slightest look easily will unclose me
though i have closed myself as fingers,
you always open petal by petal myself as Spring opens
(touching skilfully, mysteriously) her first rose

or if your wish be to close me, i and
my life will shut very beautifully, suddenly,
as when the heart of this flower imagines
the snow carefully everywhere descending;

nothing which we are to perceive in this world equals
the power of your intense fragility: whose texture
compels me with the colour of its countries
rendering death and forever with each breathing.

(i do not know what it is about you that closes
and opens; only something in me understands
the voice of your eyes is deeper than all roses)
nobody, not even the rain, has such small hands.

e. e. cummings

frail: weak
petal: part of a flower head
fragility: something fragile is easily broken
rendering: showing

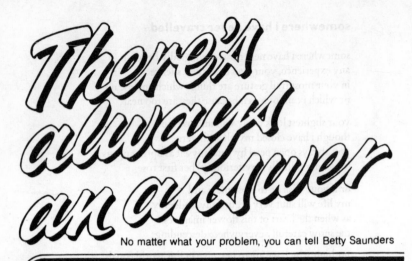

No matter what your problem, you can tell Betty Saunders

My husband is so jealous

My husband is a good, kind, generous man, but he seems unable to trust me out of his sight. He was let down in his first marriage and appears to be waiting for it to happen again. If I plan to go shopping alone he makes some excuse to come, too. He's a very keen fisherman, but he refuses to go unless I absolutely promise to stay at home. As I like him to have a hobby, I agree, but even then he tells me he may ring up while he is out — though, in fact, he rarely does.

What can I do? I love him and I have no intention of being unfaithful, but I feel like a prisoner in my own home.

Your husband seems to be in real need of patience and understanding. He's rather like a child who keeps calling downstairs to make sure his mother has not left him. But, naturally, you cannot go on being a prisoner.

I should make a particular point of always telling him where you are going, so that he could, perhaps, come and pick you up from there, or ring you at a friend's house. After a while, it's very likely he won't bother

Clearly there is nothing personal in his suspicion. It's life he mistrusts, not you, so be prepared for an improvement to come gradually, not all at once.

(*Hers*)

let down: deceived, betrayed
keen: enthusiastic

"... and, my dear, jealous!"

(*Punch*)

One flesh

Lying apart now, each in a separate bed,
He with a book, keeping the light on late,
She like a girl dreaming of childhood,
All men elsewhere – it is as if they wait
Some new event: the book he holds unread,
Her eyes fixed on the shadows overhead.

Tossed up like flotsam from a former passion,
How cool they lie. They hardly ever touch,
Or if they do it is like a confession
Of having little feeling – or too much.
Chastity faces them, a destination
For which their whole lives were a preparation.

Strangely apart, yet strangely close together,
Silence between them like a thread to hold
And not wind in. And time itself's a feather
Touching them gently. Do they know they're old,
These two who are my father and my mother
Whose fire from which I came has now grown cold?

Elizabeth Jennings

flotsam: broken pieces of wood, etc., floating on the sea
chastity: life without sex

Feiffer

70

Good marriages

I know some good marriages. Second marriages mostly. Marriages where both people have outgrown the bullshit of me-Tarzan, you-Jane and are just trying to get through their days by helping each other, being good to each other, doing the chores as they come up and not worrying too much about who does what. Some men reach that delightfully relaxed state of affairs about age forty or after a couple of divorces. Maybe marriages are best in middle age. When all the nonsense falls away and you realize you have to love one another because you're going to die anyway.

(Erica Jong, *Fear of Flying*)

bullshit: (slang) nonsense
me–Tarzan, you–Jane: behaving in exaggeratedly masculine and feminine ways (like the characters in the Tarzan films)
chores: housework

*"I'll say this much for my Bertha—
she's always tried to make marriage exciting . . ."*

(Punch)

George and Martha

[In his famous play *Who's Afraid of Virginia Woolf?*, Edward Albee shows a couple, George and Martha, who need each other and destroy each other at the same time. In the following scene, Martha explains to one of the other characters, Nick, how she really feels about George.]

MARTHA: ... There is only one man in my life who has ever ... made me happy. Do you know that? One!

NICK: The ... the what-do-you-call-it? ... uh ... the lawn mower, or something?

MARTHA: No; I'd forgotten him. But when I think about him and me it's almost like being a voyeur. Hunh. No; I didn't mean him; I meant George, of course. (*No response from* NICK) Uh ... George; my husband.

NICK (*disbelieving*): You're kidding.

MARTHA: Am I?

NICK: You must be. Him?

MARTHA: Him.

NICK: (*as if in on a joke*): Sure; sure.

MARTHA: You don't believe it.

NICK (*mocking*): Why, of course I do.

MARTHA: You always deal in appearances?

NICK (*derisively*): Oh, for God's sake ...

MARTHA: ... George who is out somewhere there in the dark. ... George who is good to me, and whom I revile; who understands me, and whom I push off; who can make me laugh, and I choke it back in my throat; who can hold me, at night, so that it's warm, and whom I will bite so there's blood; who keeps learning the games we play as quickly as I can change the rules; who can make me happy and I do not wish to be happy, and yes I do wish to be happy. George and Martha: sad, sad, sad.

NICK (*echoing, still not believing*): Sad.

MARTHA: ... whom I will not forgive for having come to rest; for having seen me and having said: yes; this will do; who has made the hideous, the hurting; the insulting mistake of loving me and must be punished for it. George and Martha: sad, sad, sad.

NICK (*puzzled*): Sad.

MARTHA: ... who tolerates, which is intolerable; who is kind, which is cruel; who understands, which is beyond comprehension. ...

NICK: George and Martha: sad, sad, sad.

(Edward Albee, *Who's Afraid of Virginia Woolf?*)

---

voyeur: person who gets sexual pleasure from watching others making love, etc.
kidding: (spoken language) teasing   *hideous:* horrible

© BRILLIANT ENTERPRISES 1972   POT-SHOTS NO. 345

WHY MUST YOU
ALWAYS UNDERMINE
MY HYSTERIA
WITH YOUR LOGIC?

Communication

Speaking of love, one problem that recurs more and more frequently
these days in books and plays and movies is the inability of people
to communicate with the people they love. Husbands and wives
who can't communicate, children who can't communicate with
their parents, and so on, and the characters in these books and plays
and so on, and in real life, I might add, spend hours bemoaning the
fact that they can't communicate. I feel that if a person can't
communicate, the very least he can do is to SHUT UP!

Tom Lehrer

recurs: is repeated
bemoaning: complaining about

Conversation at breakfast

*A country house, with two chairs and a table laid for breakfast at the centre of the
stage. These will later be removed and the action will be focused on the scullery
on the right and the study on the left, both indicated with a minimum of scenery
and props. A large well kept garden is suggested at the back of the stage with*

flower beds, trimmed hedges, etc. The garden gate, which cannot be seen by the audience, is off right.

FLORA *and* EDWARD *are discovered sitting at the breakfast table.* EDWARD *is reading the paper.*

FLORA: Have you noticed the honeysuckle this morning?

EDWARD: The what?

FLORA: The honeysuckle.

EDWARD: Honeysuckle? Where?

FLORA: By the back gate, Edward.

EDWARD: Is that honeysuckle? I thought it was . . . convolvulus, or something.

FLORA: But you know it's honeysuckle.

EDWARD: I tell you I thought it was convolvulus.

[*Pause.*]

FLORA: It's in wonderful flower.

EDWARD: I must look.

FLORA: The whole garden's in flower this morning. The clematis. The convolvulus. Everything. I was out at seven. I stood by the pool.

EDWARD: Did you say – that the convolvulus was in flower?

FLORA: Yes.

EDWARD: But good God, you just denied there was any.

FLORA: I was talking about the honeysuckle.

EDWARD: About the what?

FLORA [*calmly*]: Edward – you know that shrub outside the toolshed . . .

EDWARD: Yes, yes.

FLORA: That's convolvulus.

EDWARD: That?

FLORA: Yes.

EDWARD: Oh.

[*Pause.*]

I thought it was japonica.

FLORA: Oh, good Lord no.

EDWARD: Pass the teapot, please.

(Harold Pinter, *A Slight Ache*)

focused: concentrated
scullery: room for washing dishes
props: objects used in a play
trimmed: cut
off: not on the stage
discovered: seen when the curtain goes up
honeysuckle, convolvulus, clematis, japonica: flowering plants
shrub: ornamental bush

(Punch)

"Gerald, think of the children."

If you dont want to have a baby you have to wear a safety belt

safety belt: seat belt in a car

Alison aged 5

The best contraceptive is a glass of water – not before, or after, but instead.

(Pakistani delegate to a birth control congress)

IF YOU'RE HAPPY PREGNANT, FINE.
IF NOT, PHONE US.

(Advertisement in London tube)

"First of all, we'll discontinue the pills."

(Punch)

The chocolates in this machine taste of rubber

(Inscription on a contraceptive machine in a men's lavatory)

Dont throw cigarette ends into The lavatory.
It makes them soggy and hard to light.

(Inscription on a lavatory door)

soggy: heavy with water

IF YOU WISH TO PUT OUT YOUR CIGARETTE IN YOUR PLATE, PLEASE NOTIFY THE WAITRESS, WHO WILL GLADLY SERVE YOUR FOOD IN AN ASHTRAY.

(Sign in a Colorado café)

"Sorry, sir — no smoking in the museum."

Ronald Searle

Smokers of the World, Unite

It can scarcely have escaped the notice of thinking men, I think, being a thinking man myself, that the forces of darkness opposed to those of us who like a quiet smoke are gathering momentum daily and starting to throw their weight about more than somewhat. Every morning I read in the papers a long article by another of those doctors who are the spearhead of the movement. Tobacco, they say, plugs up the arteries and lowers the temperature of the body extremities, and if you reply that you like your arteries plugged up and are all for having the temperature of your body extremities lowered, especially during the summer months, they bring up that cat again.

The cat to which I allude is the one that has two drops of nicotine placed on its tongue and instantly passes beyond the veil. 'Look,' they say. 'I place two drops of nicotine on the cat's tongue. Now watch it wilt.' I can't see the argument. Cats, as Charles Stuart Calverley said, may have had their goose cooked by tobacco juice, but are we to deprive ourselves of all our modest pleasures just because indulgence in them would be harmful to some cat which is probably a perfect stranger?

Take a simple instance such as occurs every Saturday on the Rugby football field. The ball is heeled out, the scrum half gathers it, and instantaneously two fourteen-stone forwards fling themselves on his person, grinding him into the mud. Must we abolish Twickenham and Murrayfield because some sorry reasoner insists that if the scrum half had been a cat he would have been squashed flatter than a Dover sole? And no use, of course, to try to drive into these morons' heads that scrum halves are not cats. Really, one feels inclined at times to give it all up and turn one's face to the wall.

It is pitiful to think that that is how these men spend their lives, putting drops of nicotine on the tongues of cats day after day after day. Slaves to a habit, is the way I look at it. But if you tell them that and urge them to pull themselves together and throw off the shackles, they just look at you with fishy eyes and mumble something about it can't be done. Of course it can be done. All it requires is will power. If they were to say to themselves 'I will not start putting nicotine on cats' tongues till after lunch' it would be a simple step to knocking off during the afternoon, and by degrees they would find that they could abstain altogether. The first cat of the day is the hard one to give up. Conquer the impulse for the after-breakfast cat, and the battle is half won.

(P. G. Wodehouse in *Punch Guide to Good Living*)

momentum: force
throw their weight about: behave in an authoritarian way
more than somewhat: a lot
spearhead: leaders
plugs up: blocks
they bring up that cat: they talk about that cat
allude: refer
passes beyond the veil: dies
wilt: fade (like a dying flower)
had their goose cooked: been killed
scrum half: a position in rugby football
fourteen-stone: very heavy (about 90 kilos)
Twickenham and Murrayfield: international rugby football grounds
sorry reasoner: illogical person
morons: idiots
pull themselves together: get control of themselves
shackles: chains
mumble: say unclearly
knocking off: (slang) giving up
abstain: give up

Common sense about smoking

It is often said, 'I know all about the risk to my health, but I think that the risk is worth it.' When this statement is true it should be accepted. Everyone has the right to choose what risks they take, however great they may be. However, often the statement really means, 'I have a nasty feeling that smoking is bad for my health, but I would rather not think about it.' With some of these people the bluff can be called and they can be asked to explain what they think the risk to their own health is. When this is done few get very far in personal terms. The bare fact that 23,000 people died of lung cancer last year in Great Britain often fails to impress an individual. When it is explained that this is the equivalent of one every twenty-five minutes or is four times as many as those killed on the roads, the significance is more apparent. The one-in-eight risk of dying of lung cancer for the man who smokes twenty-five or more cigarettes a day may be better appreciated if an analogy is used. If, when you boarded a plane, the girl at the top of the steps were to welcome you aboard with the greeting, 'I am pleased that you are coming with us – only one in eight of our planes crashes,' how many would think again, and make other arrangements? Alternatively, the analogy of Russian Roulette may appeal. The man smoking twenty-five or more a day runs the same risk between the ages of thirty and sixty as another who buys a revolver with 250 chambers and inserts one live bullet and on each of his birthdays spins the chamber, points the revolver at his head, and pulls the trigger. One of the difficulties in impressing these facts on people, is that, despite the current epidemic of lung cancer, because it is a disease which kills relatively quickly, there are many who have as yet no experience of it among their family or friends.

Christopher Wood

the bluff can be called: their defences can be broken down
Russian Roulette: kind of 'suicide game' in which someone puts one bullet into a revolver, spins the chambers, points it at his head and pulls the trigger – with one chance in six of killing himself

---

Cigarette smoking does not make you look more mature. It just makes you look older – and smelly as well.

(Dr Alfred Yarrow, Department of Health)

"Give up smoking? Why?"

(Punch)

Has smallpox disappeared for ever?

Smallpox, the most devastating and feared pestilence in human history, is making its last stand in two remote areas of Ethiopia, one in the desert and one in the mountains. As of the end of August only five villages had experienced cases in the preceding eight weeks. More important, the onset of the last known case was on August 9. Because man is the only known reservoir of the smallpox virus, the disease should be eliminated forever when the last infected person recovers. Right now more than 1,000 Ethiopian health workers, together with 10 epidemiologists of the World Health Organization, are combing the countryside to make sure no more cases exist. If they discover one, the victim will be isolated under 24-hour guard and everyone who has been in contact with him will be vaccinated. An effort will be made to trace the chain of infection back to a previously known, contained outbreak. For two years after the last case is recorded the search will continue for additional outbreaks. If none is found, and if a WHO international commission can be satisfied that the search has been thorough, smallpox will be declared to have been eradicated from the earth. It will be the first such achievement in medical history.

(Donald A. Henderson, *Scientific American*, October 1976)

pestilence: serious epidemic disease
onset: beginning
reservoir: store

combing: searching very thoroughly
eradicated: wiped out, eliminated

Crank medicine becomes respectable

In treating disease, the frontier between 'establishment' medicine and 'alternative' medicine seems to be shifting. In recent years, certain beliefs and views that seemed to be part of 'crank' territory have moved across into the hallowed regions of accepted practice. So what's next? What are the ideas which we currently pooh pooh which by next year we'll have begun to accept?

YOU asked Michael van Straten — who practises acupuncture, osteopathy, naturopathy and herbalism—to report on past developments, and to predict what may be on the way.

IT IS undoubtedly true that some of yesterday's fringe therapies are becoming part of everyday medical routine, and I believe that a number of today's unorthodox ideas will tomorrow appear in the textbooks as standard practice.

For example, acupuncture has existed in China for seven thousand years, the earliest writing dates back to 3000 BC, to the Yellow Emperor. But in the West acupuncture was regarded as mumbo jumbo until President Nixon's visit to China. One of the American newsmen, James Reston, was taken ill on the tour and while in hospital witnessed an operation under acupuncture anaesthesia. He described what he had seen in the *New York Times* and started a story of controversy.

Allegations of hypnosis, auto-suggestion and even the secret use of pain-killing drugs poured from the medical Press, until the American Medical Association was invited to send an investigating team to China. Doctors were forced by the evidence of their own eyes to accept acupuncture anaesthesia; even so, most still disregard its therapeutic value.

It's easy to understand the scientists' caution, as Aldous Huxley has pointed out: 'That a needle stuck into one's foot should improve the functioning of one's liver is obviously incredible, it makes no sense. Within our system of explanation there is no reason why the needle prick should be followed by an improvement of liver function. Therefore we say it can't happen. The only trouble with this argument is that as a matter of empirical fact, it does happen.'

But acupuncture has proven uses in the treatment of many diseases—from drug addiction to migraine, from eczema and psoriasis to high blood pressure, from arthritis and rheumatism to ulcers. But widespread acceptance of this lies in the future. The development of sensitive electronic apparatus which can trace the course of the Chinese 'meridians,' or lines of energy flow, and which can also measure changes in current when specific points are pricked, may help.

Another therapy which is now crossing into established practice is naturopathy.

Again it's very old. In 1550 BC the Ebers Papyrus gave a remedy for night-blindness—'roasted ox liver crushed to a paste.' This remedy is certain to have been effective, because of the Vitamin A content of the liver and its relation to night-blindness. But that relationship is a discovery of recent times.

(*The Observer*)

crank medicine: kinds of medical treatment based on 'wild' theories not accepted as scientifically proved by orthodox doctors
establishment medicine: orthodox medicine
alternative: the same as crank
shifting: moving
hallowed: greatly respected
pooh pooh: laugh at, treat as ridiculous
YOU: a regular column in *The Observer*
acupuncture: treatment by sticking needles into the body at certain points
osteopathy: treatment by manipulation (handling) of the bones and muscles
naturopathy: treatment of disease by 'natural' methods, including attention to diet and general way of life
herbalism: treatment by plants
fringe therapies: forms of treatment which are 'on the edge' of orthodox medicine
mumbo jumbo: nonsense
anaesthesia: making the body insensitive to pain in order to operate
controversy: disagreement
therapeutic value: value in curing disease
papyrus: old Egyptian manuscript

(Punch)

"Good morning, madam. Do you have any children that want to be doctors?"

83

The kiss of life

Mouth-to-mouth method of artificial respiration

In an adult –
- open your mouth wide and take a deep breath;
- pinch the casualty's nostrils together with your fingers
- seal your lips round his mouth;
- blow into his lungs until the chest rises (Fig. 52).
- then remove your mouth and watch the chest fall;
- repeat and continue inflations at the natural rate of breathing

Figure 52: Seal lips round mouth and blow into lungs.

In an infant or young child –
Modify the foregoing instructions by *gently* blowing into his mouth and if necessary seal your lips round his mouth and nose.

Give the first four inflations as rapidly as possible to saturate the blood with oxygen.

(The St John Ambulance Association and Brigade, *The Essentials of First Aid*)

respiration: breathing
nostrils: nose-holes
seal: close tightly
inflation: blowing in air
saturate: fill

How to keep fit

Exercise Eight. Push-ups

Start Lie face down, legs straight and together, toes turned under, hands directly under shoulders.

Push up from hands and toes until arms are fully extended.
Keep body and legs in a straight line. Return to touch chest to floor and repeat.

Count Each time chest touches floor count one.

Exercise Ten. Run and semi-squat jumps

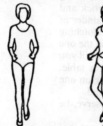

Start Stand erect, feet together, arms at sides.

Starting with left leg, run in place raising feet at least six inches from floor.

Count Each time left foot touches floor counts one.
After each fifty counts do ten semi-squat jumps.

Semi-squat jumps Drop to a half crouch position with hands on knees and arms straight. Keep back as straight as possible, one foot slightly ahead of the other. Jump to upright position with body straight and feet leaving floor. Reverse position of feet before landing, return to half crouch, and repeat.

(Physical Fitness)

squat: position of 'sitting on one's heels'

Before your very eyes:
the impossible in action

Take a pile of bricks – about a dozen, or possibly a few more. Pile them up on the table, grip the top brick in your right hand and, thus propped, raise yourself, upside down, into the air. You are now balanced on one hand on a pile of bricks, your body forming, so to speak, an extension of the pile. Your feet should be together, the toes outstretched and pointing at the ceiling.

I should have said, incidentally, that you are to wear a simple tunic and a pair of light trousers, not too baggy.

Now comes the difficult bit. Gripping the brick on which your entire weight rests, lift it (and therefore, yourself) a few inches into the air. You are now, if you have followed me thus far, suspended upside down just over a pile of bricks, clutching one in your right hand. After a fairly short time, you will, owing to the force of gravity, begin to descend, brick and head foremost and feet last, on to the remainder of the pile. As you do so, use the brick you are clutching to knock away the next brick down. Land on the one below it. Repeat the process, brick by brick, until you are standing on one hand, on a brick, on a table. Throw the brick away; you are now standing on one hand on a table. Lower yourself to the ground.

Quite so; it cannot, as you so rightly observe, be done.

As you say with considerable justice, it is not that it is very difficult; it is literally impossible.

Very well; if it is impossible, don't do it. Do the following instead; you will need four friends, and I had better warn you that you would be well advised to pick four very trustworthy ones.

Go and stand on one end of a seesaw, on the other end of which there is nothing, so that your end is resting on the ground. Arrange for a second seesaw to be placed immediately in front of yours, with one of your friends standing on the end nearer you, so that he, too, is on the ground. Beyond the 'up' end of his seesaw, cause to be erected a simple scaffolding structure, rather like a giant cakestand, some 14 feet high. Have your second and third friends climb up and stand on the top of it. Stop the music. Did I not mention that there was music? So sorry, there is, and you stop it at this point.

You stop it *apparently* to heighten the dramatic effect of what you are about to do, but *in fact* so that you can make quite sure, by listening very hard indeed, that your fourth friend has entered and is standing immediately behind you; he should be carrying a long pole, and balanced on the end of the pole should be an armchair.

Now; the two gentlemen on the cakestand should link arms and jump off it, landing on the 'up' end of the second seesaw. This will go down with considerable force, and the gentleman at the other end will be shot into the air. Pausing only to turn a back somersault, he will come down, with even greater force, on the 'up' end of *your* seesaw; events, as far as you are concerned, will now proceed to take place with dangerously bewildering rapidity. You will be shot into the air; you will turn *three* back somersaults, and you will land, in a sitting position, in the armchair held at the top of the long pole by your friend behind you. (And do be sure, before starting, that you have made arrangements to get down; it is a *very* long pole.)

Your response is easily predictable: that's impossible too. And so it is. . . . And yet I have seen these things done, and many more like them. Nor was it necessary for me to go, in order to see them, to the place where Alph, the sacred river, ran, through caverns measureless to man, down to a sunless sea. Indeed, I had to go no further than the Coliseum Theatre in St Martin's Lane, where all the things that I have described, and a number of things impossible to describe, have been taking place nightly, and twice on Saturdays. These things are in the repertoire of the Chinese Acrobatic Theatre of Shanghai.

(Bernard Levin in *The Times*)

propped: supported
tunic: close-fitting jacket
baggy: loose
thus far: so far, up to now
clutching: holding tightly
seesaw: plank of wood supported in the middle and arranged so that when one end goes up the other goes down, usually found in children's playgrounds
scaffolding structure: building made from wooden or metal poles (often used by builders working on the outside of a house)
turn a somersault: turn over in the air
bewildering: confusing
rapidity: speed
where Alph, the sacred river, ran . . . : quotation from the poem 'Kubla Khan' by Coleridge

Ask the deaf if silence is golden.

You can be very sure that anyone who tells you silence is golden, isn't deaf.

It's not just a matter of not hearing. Deafness can also mean not being able to learn. Or read and write. Or communicate. Or do anything fulfilling with your life.

The RNID aims to help **all** who suffer from deafness to overcome these problems. We provide a special school for children, a hostel for young adults, residential homes for the elderly. We run special laboratories, a welfare service and the world's largest information service devoted entirely to deafness. Unfortunately, it all takes a lot of money.

We depend on donations, covenants and bequests to continue our work. We can't make silence golden but, with your contribution, we can at least go on relieving some of the problems.

So please give us something soon.

No stamp needed.

The Royal National Institute for the Deaf
Room 4A, FREEPOST, London
WC1 6BR (Tel : 01-387 8033)

The Royal National Institute for the

deaf

helps deaf people to live with deafness

(Patron : HRH The Duke of Edinburgh KG)

(Advertisement in *The Observer*)

donations: gifts
covenants: agreements to pay regular sums of money
bequests: money left after death

Long silence

From Mr Sidney Campion

Sir, Well on the way to 85, and needing a new hearing aid to cope with my increasing deafness, I applied for one of the new free ear-level aids supplied by the Government. I was told that I could not have one until I was 90. Fair enough if the supply position is that bad, but I am now wondering how, in the meantime, I am going to hear the melodious notes of the golden trumpet calling me home?

Yours sincerely,

SIDNEY R. CAMPION,
13 Argyle Court,
Argyle Road,
Southport, Lancashire,
September 30.

(*The Times*)

hearing aid: device used by deaf people to help them hear better
cope with: deal with

*"That's that, I'm afraid. It's incurable.
Have a nice death."*

(*Punch*)

DEATH IS NATURE'S WAY OF TELLING US TO SLOW DOWN

(Inscription on a wall in Oxford)

Just living

From Mr Monja Danischewsky

Sir, As if the human race has not enough troubles to bedevil it, we make things worse by continuing to warn each other of the fatal consequences of our everyday habits. Smoking gives us cancer; butter clogs our arteries; eggs ruin our livers; sweets rot our teeth; coffee gives us insomnia; brandy brings on heart attacks; sex drives us mad; no sex drives us madder—and so on.

Could we not rationalize the situation into one all embracing statement: *Just Living Kills You In The End?* A Government health warning to that effect could be made to appear, by law, on all birth certificates.

Yours faithfully,

M. DANISCHEWSKY,
Tilford House Farm,
Tilford,
Farnham,
Surrey.

(*The Times*)

bedevil it: cause it trouble
clogs: blocks
rationalize: organize tidily

Isn't it grand?

Look at the coffin, with golden handles
Isn't it grand, boys, to be bloody well dead?
Let's not have a sniffle, let's have a bloody good
    cry,
And always remember, the longer you live, the
    sooner you bloody well die.

Look at the flowers, all bloody withered,
Isn't it grand, boys, to be bloody well dead?
Let's not . . .

Look at the mourners, bloody great hypocrites,
Isn't it grand, boys, to be bloody well dead?
Let's not . . .

Look at the preacher, bloody nice fellow,
Isn't it grand, boys, to be bloody well dead?
Let's not . . .

Look at the widow, bloody great female,
Isn't it grand, boys, to be bloody well dead?
Let's not . . .

(Traditional)

coffin: the box that dead people are buried in
let's not have a sniffle: let's not cry just a little
withered: dying
mourners: the people who attend a funeral and show their sorrow
preacher: priest

Two epitaphs

Lovely Pamela, who found
One sure way to get around
Goes to bed beneath this stone,
Early, sober, and alone.

Richard Usborne

When you go home
Tell them of us, and say
For your tomorrow
We gave our today.

(Memorial to the Allied dead at Kohima, where the Japanese invasion
of India was halted during the Second World War)

epitaph: inscription on a gravestone

Two friends

I have something to tell you.
I'm listening.
I'm dying.
I'm sorry to hear.
I'm growing old.
It's terrible.
It is, I thought you should know.
Of course and I'm sorry. Keep in touch.
I will and you too.
And let me know what's new.
Certainly, though it can't be much.
And stay well.
And you too.
And go slow.
And you too.

David Ignatow

It has been a good time for me

[In this recorded conversation with a friend, Alison Willson described her reactions to the news that she was going to die of cancer. The conversation took place five months before her death.]

Firstly, I told myself, 'The thing has happened. However much you fuss, and scream, and yell, it's not going to change.' I realised I'd got to discipline myself. Another thing was, I remembered the vicar of a church I used to go to saying that this kind of thing was often much harder for the relatives than for the patient. So here there was scope for me to do something positive.

Thirdly, just before I left the hospital, I came across two young women in their thirties, both with small children and both with cancer. I thought, well, what am I worrying about, because my children are grown up and independent. If I can get this right for myself and make some sort of peace with it, then the people who love me will also accept it and this needn't be too bad a time.

Of course, it wasn't as simple as that. When I came out of hospital I found I was getting it wrong with quite a lot of people, because they didn't look at it the same way as I did. And again, I think if you're going to die around the age of 50, far more people are involved than if you're dying when you're really old. You know, it's fairly threatening to people of your own age; they see you in the middle of a fairly busy life suddenly stopping – and they find it unacceptable. This business again of getting them to give me permission to die. . . .

Several of my friends still feel very angry and bitter about it and just won't accept it. In consequence they tell me I shouldn't accept it. I get all these stories about these heroic people who have organ after organ removed and say, I'm not

going to die, I'm going to live; and they go on, year after year. It makes me feel I'm being terribly feeble. I feel rather guilty, as if what they're saying is, well, you're not trying hard enough.

I can't really see what else I could be doing. I'm very confused about all this. I don't quite understand what I ought to do. Well, I suppose one could be a Chichester and rush across the Atlantic in a boat. But you know, really, I'm too tired for that. I think what I want to say to people is that if you're in this situation it isn't nearly as bad as people who try and put themselves in your position think it is.

For one thing, other people come to it cold, whereas I've been doing my homework on it for the last two years. I've got used to the idea and have come to the point of acceptance gradually. The other thing is that they're feeling well and vigorous, with lots of things they're in the middle of doing. But I am actually getting very tired and don't feel very well.

The fact that I can't drive my car and am generally having to cut down my activities isn't as bad for me as they think it is. I try to get this through to people, and it seems to . relieve their anxiety a bit. My friends are beginning to accept what is happening and 'come along with me.'

It's been a time for thinking about relationships and sorting out those which weren't very satisfactory. Also, to a large extent, the pressure is off. If you're going to die, you don't really have to do much. It's rather a relief if you're not feeling

93

well. I've been very happy these last six months.

I used to think that if you knew you were dying there would be a great black pall over everything, and nothing could be of any value. But it isn't like that. In some ways, even, you get increased appreciation of things. Colours are brighter and little pleasures mean more. You almost get another dimension.

I feel that if I hadn't understood what was happening, and come to terms with it, this would have been lost. So if you asked me whether I would rather have a coronary or what I've got, I would rather have this because I've had all this good time. And I feel sad because other people might have it, but miss it – because they aren't allowed to come to terms with what's going to happen,

or don't feel able to, and this is such a waste.

I 90 per cent believe in God, and I think that if God exists, I'm almost convinced He's on my side because, if He wasn't, I don't think I could possibly feel as I do.

If He's on my side, then, on the other side of dying, it should be all right; it may even be very good. I don't think God is a punishing God and although there are plenty of reasons why He shouldn't be on my side, I still think it's going to be all right. It may be very good and there may even be joy.

On the other hand, if God doesn't exist, then the alternative is surely like being asleep; and being asleep is all right. So really I don't think that I can lose.

(Alison Willson in *The Observer*)

fuss: complain, express anxiety
scope: opportunity
feeble: weak
Chichester: a man who sailed alone across the Atlantic
come to it cold: come to it unprepared, are taken by surprise
pall: cloud
coronary: heart attack
come to terms with: come to understand and accept

Two women

Two women in their seventies, in a Midland country town, reconstruct
the events surrounding the death of a husband.

'He got killed when he was fifty-nine, didn't he, Win?'
  'Yes he was fifty-nine.'
  'He was fifty-nine.'
  'You were with him weren't you?'
  'I was with him.'
  'Tree wasn't it?'
  'He was felling trees you see. And you should never fell a tree, not when
the sap's rising. And this was in May, wasn't it? You see. And instead of it
going that way, away from him, it came back and hit him that way. And
fetched him down.'
  'Broke the ladder in two.'
  'Branch fell on the ground . . . hit the ground . . . the rotten end broke
off . . . went up in the air . . . came down right across Joe's body.'
  'Fractured pelvis he had.'
  'Fractured pelvis he had, and three broken ribs.'
  'Penetrated lungs.'
  'And penetrated lungs. He lived three days after it.'
  'It happened on the Wednesday, and he died on the Saturday morning.
Well, Saturday dinner-time.'
  [The two women put questions to each other in order to elicit facts that
both are thoroughly familiar with. It is like a fixed scenario. The details
surrounding the event are recounted with great circumstantial intention,
and trivialities take on a momentous importance: no Wednesday, no
Saturday could ever be quite the same again, saturated as they are with the
panic and shock of the accident that killed her husband. In their
reconstruction of the past, the old use an almost incantatory repetitiousness;
a feeling that if they do not alter a single feature of such painful experience
the true explanation and significance of it may reveal itself to them.]

(Jeremy Seabrook, *Loneliness*)

felling: cutting down
sap: the 'juice' inside a tree
fractured: broken
pelvis: the frame of bone which links the legs to the bottom of the backbone
elicit: draw out
scenario: screen-play, film-script
trivialities: unimportant details
momentous: full of meaning
saturated: full
incantatory: as in a religious service

Do not go gentle into that good night

[Dylan Thomas wrote this poem when his father was dying.]

Do not go gentle into that good night,
Old age should burn and rave at close of day;
Rage, rage against the dying of the light.

Though wise men at their end know dark is right,
Because their words had forked no lightning they
Do not go gentle into that good night.

Good men, the last wave by, crying how bright
Their frail deeds might have danced in a green bay,
Rage, rage against the dying of the light.

Wild men who caught and sang the sun in flight,
And learn, too late, they grieved it on its way,
Do not go gentle into that good night.

Grave men, near death, who see with blinding sight
Blind eyes could blaze like meteors and be gay,
Rage, rage against the dying of the light.

And you, my father, there on the sad height,
Curse, bless, me now with your fierce tears, I pray.
Do not go gentle into that good night.
Rage, rage against the dying of the light.

Dylan Thomas

rave: shout wildly
forked no lightning: not made lightning flash
the last wave by: when the last wave has passed
frail: weak
grieved it on its way: mourned its departure

It was all very tidy

When I reached his place,
The grass was smooth,
The wind was delicate,
The wit well timed,
The limbs well formed,
The pictures straight on the wall:
It was all very tidy.

He was cancelling out
The last row of figures,
He had his beard tied up in ribbons,
There was no dust on his shoe,
Everyone nodded:
It was all very tidy.

Music was not playing,
There were no sudden noises,
The sun shone blandly,
The clock ticked:
It was all very tidy.

'Apart from and above all this,'
I reassured myself,
'There is now myself.'
It was all very tidy.

Death did not address me,
He had nearly done:
It was all very tidy.

They asked, did I not think
It was all very tidy?

I could not bring myself
To laugh, or untie
His beard's neat ribbons,
Or jog his elbow,
Or whistle, or sing,
Or make disturbance.
I consented, frozenly,
He was unexceptionable:
It was all very tidy.

    Robert Graves

blandly: in a self-satisfied way
he had nearly done: he had nearly finished
jog: knock
he was unexceptionable: there was nothing about him to criticize

It was all very untidy

Not until I left home did I ever live in a house where the rooms were clear
and carpeted, where corners were visible and window-seats empty, and
where it was possible to sit on a kitchen chair without first turning it up and
shaking it. Our Mother was one of those obsessive collectors who spend all
their time stuffing the crannies of their lives with a ballast of wayward
objects. She collected anything that came to hand, she never threw anything
away, every rag and button was carefully hoarded as though to lose it would
imperil us all. Two decades of newspapers, yellow as shrouds, was the dead
past she clung to, the years saved for my father, maybe something she
wished to show him. . . . Other crackpot symbols also littered the house:
chair-springs, boot-lasts, sheets of broken glass, corset-bones, picture-frames,
fire-dogs, top-hats, chess-men, feathers, and statues without heads. Most of
these came on the tides of unknowing, and remained as though left by a
flood. But in one thing – old china – Mother was a deliberate collector, and
in this had an expert's eye.

Old china to Mother was gambling, the bottle, illicit love, all stirred up
together; the sensuality of touch and the ornament of a taste she was born to
but could never afford. She hunted old china for miles around, though she
hadn't the money to do so; haunted shops and sales with wistful passion,
and by wheedling, guile and occasional freaks of chance carried several fine
pieces home.

(Laurie Lee, *Cider with Rosie*)

stuffing the crannies: filling up the little corners
ballast: weight put into an unloaded ship to keep it steady
wayward: undisciplined
hoarded: saved
imperil: endanger
decade: ten years
shroud: sheet used to wrap a dead body
clung: held tightly
crackpot: (slang) mad
boot-lasts: foot-shaped pieces of metal used for repairing shoes
fire-dogs: metal objects put at the side of a coal fire, to hold the shovel, poker, brush,
etc.
gambling: betting money on cards, horses, etc.
illicit: unlawful
haunted: waited around
wistful: sad, regretful
wheedling: talking persuasively
guile: cunning
freaks: unusual events

House for sale

£1,990. Long 33 yrs lse. G.R. only £6 10s. Tory Senior Bank Official & former girl fencing champion of Ireland forced sacrifice vile little PUTNEY Victorian villa. The river can be seen from the decrepit balcony. 5 dilapidated rms, kitchen, sep scullery, a bathrm which has the air of not having been used for decades & a large framed portrait of Queen Alexandra. Flags bravely flower in tiny back garden. The brick air-raid shelter is about the only decent modern construction around the place. View Sun: Uplands 0424.

(E. H. Brooks & Son advertisement)

lse: lease (right to occupy a house for a number of years)
G.R.: ground rent (small annual payment by the leaseholder to the owner)
Tory: Conservative
fencing: kind of sword-fighting for sport
sacrifice: sell very cheap
vile: horrible

Putney: suburb of London
villa: suburban house
decrepit: in a bad condition
dilapidated: the same as *decrepit*
sep: separate
scullery: washing-up room
flags: irises
air-raid shelter: bomb shelter

Accom. Vacant

SW4. Small bed-sit in quiet house, cooking facilities, share bath & w.c. 622 5734.

HAMPSTEAD. Sgle bed-sit. for young, working m. grad. £8.50 p.w. Tel. 435 8109.

SHARE LARGE W. HAMPSTEAD FLAT with 1 male (University lecturer). Own room, lounge, kitchen, bathroom, TV, phone etc. Pleasant area, £70 p.c.m. Phone 435 4247 or 836 5454 ext. 2392 (day).

TRANSLATOR, (f), offers attractive room. Kew Gardens, use k.&b. Suit prof. woman. Box 5618.

WINTER LET OF COTTAGE in .idyllic countryside, South Wales. Huge lounge, 2 bedrooms, on edge of forestry commission. £22 p.w. inclusive heating, cheaper if paid in one lump sum. 01-883 4039.

(Advertisements in *New Statesman*)

bed-sit: bed-sitting room
sgle: single
m. grad.: male graduate
p.w.: per week
p.c.m.: per calendar month
f.: female
k. & b.: kitchen and bathroom

prof.: professional (lawyer, doctor, etc.)
idyllic: very beautiful and peaceful
forestry commission: (land belonging to) the government department that looks after Britain's forests
in one lump sum: all at the same time

35 NORREYS AVENUE
OFF ABINGDON ROAD,
OXFORD.

Situated about 1 mile south of Carfax, this terraced house is constructed of brick, stone and slate and has a freshly rendered front elevation.

The house has modern 13 amp. electrical ring mains, a modern bathroom and a spacious breakfast kitchen.

Arranged on two floors, the accommodation comprises:

PORCH

HALL

LOUNGE: 13'6" into bay x 11'9". Fireplace (panelled in).
                  13 amp. power point.

DINING ROOM: 11'5" x 9'8". Tiled fireplace. 13 amp. power point.

BREAKFAST KITCHEN: 17'9" x 9'10". Attractive tiled fireplace with back
                  boiler fitted. 2 13 amp. power points. Cooker
                  panel. Sink unit. Venetian blinds as fitted. Door
                  to garden.

                  FIRST FLOOR

LANDING

BEDROOM 1.   15' x 13'6" into bay. Built-in cupboard. 13 amp.
                  power point.

BEDROOM 2.   11'6" x 9'7". Built-in cupboard. 13 amp. power
                  point.

BEDROOM 3.   10'6" x 9'9". Hot water tank with fitted immersion
                  heater. 13 amp. power point.

BATHROOM.   Panelled bath (h and c). Pedestal hand basin
                  (h and c). Low flush W.C.

                  OUTSIDE

GARDENS   with lawn, flower and rose beds. Fuel bunker and
                  shed.

                  ALL MAIN SERVICES ARE AVAILABLE
                  (Gas not connected at present)

RATES: Rateable value £70. Current rates payable: £23.12.6. per
                  half year including water
PRICE: .... £4,000 .... FREEHOLD

(House-agent's description of a house for sale)

terraced house: house that forms part of a connected row
slate: a blue–grey stone used for roofing
rendered: given a first coat of plaster
front elevation: front

amp.: ampere (unit of electric current)
ring mains: system of electrical connections
porch: covered doorway
13′ 6″: 13 feet 6 inches (12 inches = 1 foot = about 30 cm)
panelled in: covered up with wood
power point: electrical socket
back boiler: kind of water heater
sink unit: sink and cupboards built together
Venetian blinds: window covers made of strips of wood or plastic
immersion heater: heater inside a water tank
panelled bath: bath with the sides covered with wooden or plastic panels
h and c: hot and cold water
low flush W.C.: lavatory with a handle, not a chain
bunker: store
freehold: the buyer becomes the absolute owner of the property

Perpendicular

Unlike the other three styles of medieval architecture, which were common to all northern Europe, Perpendicular was a purely English discovery and its masterpieces cannot be paralleled anywhere abroad. This style, which attained to its fullest development in the second half of the fifteenth century, was the logical outcome of a curious passion for height, operating within the conventions of the Decorated style of the previous age. All the elements of

the latter style are still here but curiously distorted and changed; the vertical lines have become fantastically prolonged and when at last they curve inwards they do so far more abruptly, giving to the resulting arch a curiously flattened form. In addition, a number of horizontal bars appear in the tracery of the windows, rendered essential by the need to provide some support for the thin perpendicular shafts. At the same time the system of vaulting grew ever more complex and it became customary to indulge in a superabundance of ribs and bosses, the majority of which fulfilled no structural purpose, until finally the system known as 'fan-vaulting' was evolved: an architectural device which arouses enormous enthusiasm on account of the difficulties it has all too obviously involved but which from an aesthetic standpoint frequently belongs to the 'Last-Supper-carved-on-a-peachstone' class of masterpiece. Externally the most remarkable features of the style were the flying buttresses, which although they occur in other methods of building, are here developed to a most fantastic pitch of ingenuity. It is as though the Perpendicular architect abhorred any unnecessary expanse of masonry and was desirous of eliminating every square inch of solid stone that was not absolutely essential to the stability of the building; even battlements which were still retained round the roof for decorative purposes were pierced and hollowed until they resembled nothing so much as a plan or map of themselves. Many of the most notable examples of the style differ from vast conservatories only in that the framework is of stone, not iron or wood and that the glass is coloured.

Nevertheless, with all its grandeur and beauty it must be admitted that Perpendicular remains, in most cases, an essentially virtuoso performance compelling an admiration that is not far removed from astonishment.

(Osbert Lancaster, *Pillar to Post*)

abruptly: suddenly
tracery: decorative pattern
shafts: thin columns
vaulting: roof-making
a superabundance of: very many, too many
ribs: lines, strips of stone
bosses: round pieces of stone sticking out
'*Last-Supper-carved-on-a-peachstone*': like carving a copy of Leonardo da Vinci's painting 'The Last Supper' on a peachstone – clever but with no artistic value
flying buttresses: a buttress is a stone support for a wall; a flying buttress touches the wall only at the top
pitch: level, height
ingenuity: complicated kind of cleverness
abhorred: hated
masonry: stone
battlements: kind of wall with spaces, found round castle roofs, from which people could shoot
conservatories: glass houses for growing plants
virtuoso: demonstrating great artistic skill

Squatters in clash with council over eviction

By Robert Parker

The proposed demolition of 49 large terrace houses in St Agnes Place, Kennington, south London, and Lambeth Borough Council's plan to turn the site into open space, at a cost of £40,000, was described yesterday as "a staggering waste of chronically short housing" by the Lambeth Self Help group. Under licence from the council it specializes in finding temporary or short-life housing for the homeless.

Trouble flared up yesterday when council workmen were sent to make 85 St Agnes Place uninhabitable.

Mrs Ruby Thompson, aged 78, the last but one council tenant in the affected houses, has lived in the basement and ground floor there for 30 years. She did not want to be rehoused.

When council officials arrived to move her and wreck the house so that squatters could not move in they found there too many of the 110 squatters who live in other houses.

About twenty squatters got into the top two unoccupied floors by means of a ladder. Police ejected three, but the rest were left there while council workmen chopped out the staircase and removed flooring in the ground floor and basement. There was much shouting and abuse and Mrs Thompson left in tears.

(The Times)

squatters: people who illegally occupy empty houses
clash: fight
eviction: throwing somebody out of the house where they live
terrace houses: houses built together in a row
staggering: astonishing
chronically short: the shortage is like a permanent disease
the last but one: the one before the last
wreck: destroy
ejected: threw out
chopped: cut with axes
abuse: insults

Telephone conversation

The price seemed reasonable, location
Indifferent. The landlady swore she lived
Off premises. Nothing remained
But self-confession. 'Madam,' I warned,
'I hate a wasted journey – I am African.'
Silence. Silenced transmission of
Pressurized good-breeding. Voice, when it came,

103

Lipstick coated, long gold–rolled
Cigarette-holder pipped. Caught I was, foully.
'HOW DARK?' . . . I had not misheard . . . 'ARE YOU LIGHT
OR VERY DARK?' Button B. Button A. Stench
Of rancid breath of public hide-and-speak.
Red booth. Red pillar-box. Red double-tiered
Omnibus squelching tar. It *was* real! Shamed
By ill-mannered silence, surrender
Pushed dumbfoundment to beg simplification.
Considerate she was, varying the emphasis –
'ARE YOU DARK? OR VERY LIGHT?' Revelation came.
'You mean – like plain or milk chocolate?'
Her assent was clinical, crushing in its light
Impersonality. Rapidly, wave-length adjusted,
I chose. 'West African sepia' – and as afterthought,
'Down in my passport.' Silence for spectroscopic
Flight of fancy, till truthfulness clanged her accent
Hard on the mouthpiece. 'WHAT'S THAT?' conceding
'DON'T KNOW WHAT THAT IS.' 'Like brunette.'
'THAT'S DARK, ISN'T IT?' 'Not altogether.
Facially, I am brunette, but, madam, you should see
The rest of me. Palm of my hand, soles of my feet
Are a peroxide blond. Friction, caused –
Foolishly, madam – by sitting down, has turned
My bottom raven black – One moment, madam!' – sensing
Her receiver rearing on the thunderclap
About my ears – 'Madam,' I pleaded, 'wouldn't you rather
See for yourself?'

Wole Soyinka

indifferent: unimportant
off premises: not in the same building
breeding: upbringing
foully: very badly
stench: stink
rancid: sour, bad
hide-and-speak: play on words referring to
the children's game called 'hide-and-seek'
booth: telephone cabin
pillar-box: letter-box
squelching: noise of something wet being
pressed or squashed

dumbfoundment: word invented by the
writer; *dumbfounded* means astonished
revelation: understanding
assent: agreement
clinical: cold, unemotional
down in my passport: written in my
passport
spectroscopic: analysing light and colours
flight of fancy: activity of imagination
clanged: made a hard noise
conceding: admitting
rearing: lifting up

Anti-German feeling

From Mr Alan Macrae

Sir, My family have recently returned to England after four and a half years in West Germany. We have two boys aged 10 and 12½ years, and a girl of eight.

All three had been at German schools in Frankfurt; the elder boy, on his own merit, attended the Goethe Gymnasium in Frankfurt, one of the best schools in Germany. The second boy and the girl both went to a local school in our part of town.

These British children were treated with every respect and kindness during their stay. They made many friends and were invited several times a week to parties or outings. Our departure was an occasion for tearful " parting parties ", and the children were showered with souvenirs and mementoes of their stay in Germany.

Imagine my disgust, when, after a few days at English schools, the children were being described as " dirty Germans ". Our girl was told that one child's mother had said she was not to talk to the German girl. The words " Hun " and " Boche " were heard in the playground.

I can only attribute this " hate "

attitude to the profusion of cheap comics which are sold in England depicting the Germans as our enemy. Apart from the literature, some of our poorer comedians depict ludicrous " Adolfs " on television, and highly inaccurate serials show the Germans as useless fools, easily deceived by British guile.

The informed German is painfully aware of this British attitude, but refrains from discussion on the subject. He refrains also to mention what a wonderful mess Britain has made of its economy since the war, or that British products need more after sales attention than any others.

If we seriously wish to help build a united Europe, our attitude towards the Germans must change. We continue to build a barrier of hate and ignorance despite the fact that the Germans are temperamentally more like us than any other nation in that continent.

In the next decade we will need friends in Europe, don't let's make enemies of those who wish to be our friends.

Yours faithfully,
ALAN MACRAE,
16 Calder Close,
Furze Platt,
Maidenhead,
Berkshire.
June 17.

(The Times)

---

on his own merit: because of his own ability
showered with: given lots of
mementoes: the same as souvenirs
Hun, Boche: insulting words for Germans
comics: children's weekly papers
depicting: showing, presenting
comedians: entertainers who make people laugh
Adolfs: Hitlers
guile: cunning
refrains from discussion: prefers not to talk

A German view of the British

From Mrs von Zugbach de Sugg

Sir, Having read Dan van der Vat's report today (November 16), I must heartily agree with the feeling in the repeated leading article of the *Frankfurter Allgemeine Zeitung*. Why should Germany pay for English economic incapability and as thanks should get mainly threats? After all why should the Germans turn the other cheek? Because they lost two wars?

I must say that I am heartily sick – living as a German married into English community – to be reminded at least twice a week through very biased films on television about the bad Nazis and nasty Germans in general. Funny that the German soldier always dies like a coward and a British or American under most heroic circumstances or through a vile attack by their enemy.

Why don't they show once a film about German women and children fleeing for thousands of miles from the approaching pillaging Russians (once their allies)? Or a film about the unbearable conditions in Russian POW camps, compared to which Colditz was a holiday camp? Or better, show a film about Germany today? A country that guilty and non-guilty, persecutor and persecuted alike, have made what it is now.

After the war they didn't sit back and birch themselves for the wrong they had done, but for once tried to do as much right as possible. They did it for us, the new generation who would like to live without a stigma. After all, would the British like to have the Boer War still drummed into their ears? And it was during this that the British invented concentration camps. You will quite rightly say that it has nothing to do with you.

And the French, are they still ashamed about the misery that Napoleon brought to other countries? You might say that that is long ago. But when will it be "long ago" for the Germans? Do you think that it was nice to have poppies staring into my face and made to feel guilty, where there is no guilt. And all that, when my whole family suffered great hardship during both World Wars, when they didn't fight anything but the evil in their own country? I am made to feel guilty, just because I am German. Isn't that race discrimination?

I don't bear a grudge against the British, who refused my grandfather entrance into this country, because of his age, and thus placed him in a concentration camp. I don't hate the Allies for throwing bombs just as indiscriminately on my family's house. I don't wear a badge for all my dead. If I did, people very likely would call me a Nazi.

I can't help the feeling that the British long for the good old days, and even if it is the war, where they were still great and a real world power. To feel great now, they have to find somebody they can call their inferior. Though they mustn't be too far removed. Thus the Germans and their past come handy to look down upon, despite their moral and economic recovery. Why else the sudden wave of newly published war papers, woman at war, music of the forties, etc.

May I remind you that these were the tactics that were used by Hitler against the Jews. The Jews were chosen as a perfect object to pick at. Hitler himself was a complex laden little man from a poor background, but towards the Jews he managed to feel superior. Moral superiority is so easy to establish. Isn't this too cheap a way out for the British? Can't you be great and forgive and forget, like a lot of Germans (and Jews are German too) had to do in their own country? It might also help you to realistically face your present problems.

I am, Sir, your obedient servant,
BETTINA VON ZUGBACH DE SUGG,
1 Falterley Road,
Wythenshawe,
Manchester.
November 16.

(*The Times*)

---

leading article: article in which a newspaper's owner or editor gives his opinions
turn the other cheek: respond non-violently to an attack
biased: unfair, one-sided
vile: disgusting
pillaging: stealing by invaders in a war
POW: prisoner of war
Colditz: a German prison camp for captured British officers, the subject of a television serial
birch themselves: punish themselves
stigma: sign of guilt
Boer War: war fought by British against Dutch settlers in South Africa at the end of the nineteenth century
poppies: imitation flowers sold on the anniversary of the end of the first world war; the money goes to support old soldiers
they mustn't be too far removed: the person mustn't be too different
come handy: (normally *come in handy*) are useful
pick at: (normally *pick on*) choose for persecution
complex laden: full of psychological problems

" WE'VE GOT JERRY ON THE RUN!"

(*Warlord*, a children's 'comic')

Jerry: (slang) German   *Huns:* (slang) Germans   *C.O.:* commanding officer
dead chuffed: (slang) very pleased   *skirmish:* small battle   *kip:* (slang) sleep

108

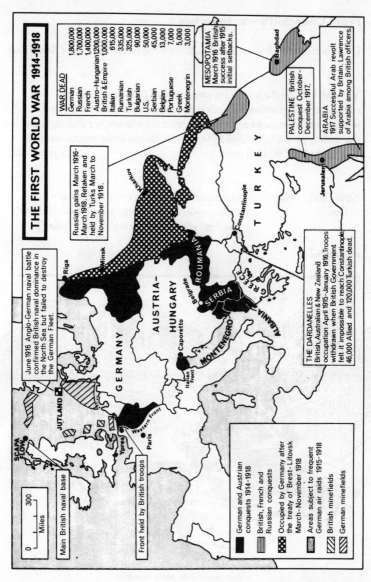

THE FIRST WORLD WAR 1914-1918

WAR DEAD	
German	1,800,000
Russian	1,700,000
French	1,400,000
Austro-Hungarian	1,200,000
British & Empire	1,000,000
Italian	615,000
Rumanian	335,000
Turkish	325,000
Bulgarian	90,000
U.S.	50,000
Serbian	45,000
Belgian	13,000
Portuguese	7,000
Greek	5,000
Montenegrin	3,000

MESOPOTAMIA March 1916 British success after 1915 initial setbacks.

PALESTINE British conquest October-December 1917.

ARABIA 1917 Successful Arab revolt supported by Britain. Lawrence of Arabia among British officers.

Russian gains March 1916-March 1918. Retaken and held by Turks March to November 1918.

June 1916 Anglo-German naval battle confirmed British naval dominance in the North Sea but failed to destroy the German Fleet.

THE DARDANELLES British, Australian & New Zealand occupation April 1915-January 1916 Troops withdrawn when British Government felt it impossible to reach Constantinople. 46,000 Allied and 120,000 Turkish dead.

Main British naval base

Front held by British troops

0 300 Miles

Kharkov

Riga

Minsk

Belgrade

Constantinople

Jerusalem

Baghdad

GERMANY

AUSTRIA-HUNGARY

ROUMANIA

SERBIA

GREECE

ALBANIA

MONTENEGRO

TURKEY

Caporetto

Italian Front

Western Front

Paris

Ypres

JUTLAND

SCAPA FLOW

- German and Austrian conquests 1914-1918
- British, French and Russian conquests
- Occupied by Germany after the treaty of Brest-Litovsk March-November 1918
- Areas subject to frequent German air raids 1915-1918
- British minefields
- German minefields

(Martin Gilbert, *British History Atlas*)

From Churchill's war speeches

I have nothing to offer but blood, toil, tears and sweat.   (*13 May 1940*)

We shall fight on the seas and oceans, we shall fight with growing confidence and growing strength in the air, we shall defend our island, whatever the cost may be, we shall fight on the beaches, we shall fight on the landing grounds, we shall fight in the fields and in the streets, we shall fight in the hills; we shall never surrender.   (*4 June 1940*)

Never in the field of human conflict was so much owed by so many to so few.   (*20 August 1940, referring to the Royal Air Force's defence of the country in the 'Battle of Britain'*)

toil: hard work

"*It says here it's the peace memorial.*"

(*Punch*)

An aggressive creature

That man is an aggressive creature will hardly be disputed. With the exception of certain rodents, no other vertebrate habitually destroys members of his own species. No other animal takes positive pleasure in the exercise of cruelty upon another of his own kind. We generally describe the most repulsive examples of man's cruelty as brutal or bestial, implying by these adjectives that such behaviour is characteristic of less highly developed animals than ourselves. In truth, however, the extremes of 'brutal' behaviour are confined to man; and there is no parallel in nature to our savage treatment of each other. The sombre fact is that we are the cruellest and most ruthless species that has ever walked the earth; and that, although we may recoil in horror when we read in newspaper or history book of the atrocities committed by man upon man, we know in our hearts that each one of us harbours within himself those same savage impulses which lead to murder, to torture and to war.

(Anthony Storr, *Human Aggression*)

rodents: family of animals which includes rats, mice, and squirrels
vertebrate: higher type of animal (distinguished by having a backbone)
species: type of animal
repulsive: disgusting

implying: suggesting
sombre: tragic
ruthless: pitiless, merciless
recoil: jump back
atrocities: cruel actions
harbours: shelters, keeps

Return of the hit men

NATO intelligence reports have revealed that a few selected Russian troops are being trained to use a new long-range rifle, code-named Dragunov.

Military chiefs realise that nuclear weapons may be too terrible, and too big, to use on a battlefield.

So they are reviving a dying art: killing one man at long range for

the destructive psychological effect it will have on his mates.

Quietly, on both sides of the Iron Curtain, they are choosing their champions, training soldiers to become the most feared and hated men at the front.

British units have always encouraged a few long-range shots. But now Army chiefs are giving the snipers a formal place in the NATO battle plan.

They will not be the traditional lone marksmen of the last two world wars, but will work on the "buddy" principle, like American TV cops.

In a two-man kill-team one will have a long-range rifle, the other a conventional weapon to watch his back, and a spy radio.

The men who go to Warminster for the sniper's course will normally be experienced NCOs who are already superlative shots.

For five weeks, they will learn how to kill—and then vanish into the countryside.

A breath of breeze, a dawn mist, the warmer air of mid-day must all be taken into account before loosing the shot that one man—the target —will never hear.

In theory, as the Russians roll towards Britain, like a steel carpet, the sniper teams will lie in wait.

When a commander pops his head from the turret of a tank it will be blown off. Recce parties would lose their leaders at the touch of a trigger. Lt.-Col. Digby Willoghby, chief sniper instructor, said: "We expect our chaps to kill quite dispassionately. There should be no hatred of the enemy or anything emotional."

Colonel Mike Hardy, commandant of the small arms wing at Warminster, has discussed the sniper problem with American experts.

"They get terribly involved with psychological tests," he said.

"We look upon a one-round kill as a simple extension of infantry kills.

"One American in the Vietnam war killed twenty-four people in one morning. It was too easy—like shooting ducks at a fun fair. He went to his CO and said he was finished; he'd lost his motivation as a sniper. It was a loss of a terribly efficient chap.

"We try not to get involved with that sort of mental problem."

(Daily Mirror)

nuclear weapons: hydrogen bombs, etc.
mates: (slang) friends
units: divisions of an army
snipers: soldiers who shoot from hiding places
buddy: (American slang) friend
cops: (slang) policemen
NCO's: non-commissioned officers (corporals and sergeants)
superlative: excellent
breeze: slight wind
turret: control tower
recce parties: reconnaissance groups (sent out to find out information)
trigger: the part of a gun which you pull with the finger in order to shoot
small arms wing: department concerned with pistols, rifles, etc.
one-round kill: kill with one bullet
CO: commanding officer

Volunteers are needed for three years National Service.

There are still people who regret the end of compulsory National Service.

In their opinion, it was the solution to everything from vandalism to the divorce rate. It taught boys to be men and it gave the Army a cheap work force.

In our opinion, it gave the Army a bad name.

It's true that we got some good men. But we also got a lot of boys who begrudged lifting a finger and lived only for demob.

Who could blame them? They didn't volunteer. They were forced labour.

We were glad to see the end of that kind of National Service, and even more pleased to start building an army of professionals.

Now we have what is considered to be one of the most efficient fighting units in the world.

We don't need conscripts because we have enough people who think the job is worth doing.

Our hope is that the day will come when every young man at the end of his education will at least ask himself whether *he* thinks the job is worth doing.

And whether he's prepared to spend three years as an Army Officer helping to do it.

So it might help if we tell you exactly what the job is.

We may as well start right at the top, however high-falutin it sounds; your job will be to defend democracy.

Because, make no mistake, it is threatened.

There are nations and there are terrorist organisations who have pledged themselves to its destruction.

We can't go into the whys and wherefores of their beliefs now, but already over half the peoples of the world live under one form of dictatorship or another.

These people do not have the rights you take for granted.

The right to vote, the right to worship as you choose, to speak your mind, to strike if you feel you're being exploited.

In short, the right to live your life as you want subject only to the wishes of the majority and the laws of the land.

This is what you might be asked to fight for; to defend even your neighbour's right to be a pacifist or a communist.

And, don't forget, because we're a member of NATO you could be asked to defend a German's rights or a Belgian's homeland.

So what do you think?

Is the job worth doing?

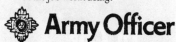 **Army Officer**

[Britain does not have compulsory military service.]

national service: military service
compulsory: obligatory (people were forced to do it)
vandalism: pointless destruction of property
begrudged lifting a finger: didn't want to do any work at all
demob: demobilization (the end of military service)
conscripts: people who are made to join the army
high-falutin': pompous, pretentious
pledged: promised
whys and wherefores: reasons
worship: practise religion

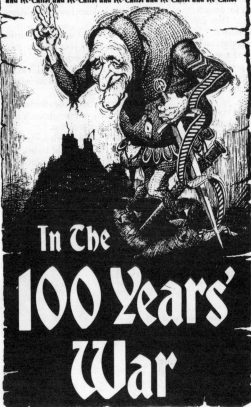

Re-Enlist
and Re-Enlist
and Re-Enlist and Re-Enlist
and Re-Enlist and Re-Enlist and Re-Enlist
and Re-Enlist and Re-Enlist and Re-Enlist and Re-Enlist
and Re-Enlist and Re-Enlist and Re-Enlist and Re-Enlist and Re-Enlist

In The
100 Years' War

(*Mad Magazine*)

enlist: join the army

Patriotism

My country, right or wrong!   (Stephen Decatur, American sailor)

Patriotism, the last refuge of a scoundrel.

(Dr Johnson, English lexicographer)

He who loves not his country, can love nothing.

(Lord Byron, English poet)

A patriot is a fool in every age.   (Alexander Pope, English poet)

My affections are first for my country, and then, generally, for all
mankind.   (Thomas Jefferson, US President)

Let our object be our country, our whole country and nothing but our
country.   (Daniel Webster, US politician)

Patriotism is your conviction that your country is superior to all others
because you were born in it.   (George Bernard Shaw, Irish dramatist)

Patriots always talk of dying for their country, and never of killing for
their country.   (Bertrand Russell, English philosopher)

A bayonet is a weapon with a worker at each end.

(British pacifist slogan)

refuge: hiding place
scoundrel: bad man
bayonet: kind of knife or sword fixed on the end of a rifle

War is, after all, the universal perversion. We are all tainted; if we cannot
experience our perversion at first hand we spend our time reading war
stories, the pornography of war; or seeing war films, the blue films of war;
or titillating our senses with the imagination of great deeds, the
masturbation of war.

(John Rae, *The Custard Boys*)

perversion: unnatural, abnormal behaviour
tainted: affected by the disease
at first hand: directly
blue films: pornographic films
titillating: exciting, stimulating

Sex and war

We adults were corrupted in infancy; we can never be free about sex matters. *Consciously*, we may be free; we may even be members of a society for the sex education of children. But I fear that *unconsciously* we remain to a large extent what conditioning in infancy made of us: haters of sex and fearers of sex.

Early in life, the child learns that the sexual sin is the great sin. Parents invariably punish most severely for an offence against sex morality. The very people who rail against Freud because he 'sees sex in everything' are the ones who have told sex stories, have listened to sex stories, have laughed at sex stories. Every man who has been in the army knows that the language of the army is a sex language. Nearly everyone likes to read the spicy accounts of divorce cases and of sex crimes in the Sunday papers, and most men tell their wives the stories they bring home from their clubs and bars ...

Now our delight in a sex story is due entirely to our own unhealthy education in sex matters. The savoury sex interest is due to repressions ... The adult condemnation of sex interest in the child is hypocritical and is humbug; the condemnation is a projection, a throwing of the guilt onto others. Parents punish severely for sex offences because they are vitally, if unhealthily, interested in sex offences.

Sex is the basis of all negative attitudes towards life ... Hate sex and you hate life. Hate sex and you cannot love your neighbour. If sex is unsatisfactory, it must go somewhere, for it is too strong an urge to be annihilated. It goes into anxiety and hate. The extreme forms of sex hate are seen in sadism. No man with a good sex life could possibly torture an animal, or torture a human, or support prisons. No sex-satisfied woman would condemn the mother of a bastard ...

The question for parents today is this: Do we want our children to be like us? If so, will society continue as it is, with rape and sex murder and unhappy marriages and unhappy children? If the answer to the first question is yes, then the same answer must be given to the second question. And both questions are the prelude to atomic destruction, because they postulate the continuance of hate and the expression of this hate in wars.

I ask moralist parents: Will you worry much about your children's sex play when the atomic bombs begin to drop? Will the virginity of your daughters assume great importance when clouds of atomic energy make life impossible?

For a parent there is no sitting on the fence, no neutrality. The choice is between guilty-secret sex or open-healthy-happy sex. If parents choose the common standard of morality, they must not complain of the misery of sex-perverted society, for it is the result of this moral code. Parents then must not hate war, for the hate of self that they give their children will express itself in war. Humanity is sick, emotionally sick, and it is sick because of this guilt and the anxiety acquired in childhood.

(Selected passages from A. S. Neill, *Summerhill*)

we . . . were corrupted: our character was spoilt
infancy: very early childhood
conditioning: training
rail against: criticize loudly
spicy: exciting because of the 'naughty' sexual element
savoury: the same as spicy
repressions: instincts which are not allowed to express themselves
humbug: dishonest, insincere
urge: instinct
annihilated: destroyed
prelude: introduction
postulate: presuppose
sitting on the fence: remaining neutral, refusing to decide for one side or the other

---

Ready? Ready!

> The world is not ready for nuclear disarmament, or any other kind of disarmament.
>
> Dr Edward Teller

In the year 2076 at last the world was ready for disarmament,
And the word went out
And from Asia and the Americas, the delegates, all four of them, came to meet in the stump of a gutted city among degraded Alps.
And the delegates from the Americas said they spoke for the entire population spread out across the hemisphere – perhaps three or four hundred people all told; and that although most of them were sick from disorders of the blood and bone marrow, those who were competent had expressed the wish to ratify the disarmament treaty.
The Asian delegates replied that on behalf of the sovereign people inhabiting the vast land mass between the Baltic and Pacific, amounting to eighty-seven persons including six children, they were equally ready to accept the treaty with only minor qualifications, these to be negotiated before final ratification, but that to all intents and purposes their attitude could be construed as an agreement in principle.
And then the delegates from the Americas asked whether anywhere in the Asias there could be spared any whole milk for the children on their side.

And the Asians replied that though their own needs were sore and pressing, they would be willing to exchange some quarts of whole milk for pints of whole blood, needed for transfusions for the six leukemic children of their own.

The exchange was agreed upon (subject to ratification on both sides of course), but before the conference adjourned two delegates collapsed and died from malnutrition, a third succumbed to sudden virulent infection to which he lacked resistance, and the fourth from internal hemorrhages induced by derangement of the clotting platelets in the blood;

And it was some time before their bodies were discovered, along with the minutes of the meeting. By then the remaining home populations were so weak that the disarmament treaty came into use automatically.

It is still in force today as I, the last human being before my species becomes extinct, write these few words for whatever intelligent beings may chance to visit this planet from dis

Norman Corwin

stump: what is left when a tree is cut down
gutted: burnt out
degraded: worn down
hemisphere: half the world
bone marrow: soft substance inside bones
ratify: give final agreement to
sovereign: self-governing
qualifications: conditions
to all intents and purposes: in practice
construed: interpreted
transfusion: giving blood
leukemic: leukemia is a blood disease
adjourned: finished its session
malnutrition: illness resulting from not having enough food
hemorrhages: loss of blood
clotting: becoming solid
minutes: record
species: type of creature

At Lunchtime: a story of love

When the busstopped suddenly to avoid damaging a mother and child in the road, the younglady in the greenhat sitting opposite was thrown across me, and not being one to miss an opportunity i started to makelove with all my body.

At first she resisted saying that it was tooearly in the morning and toosoon after breakfast and that anyway she found me repulsive. But when i explained that this being a nuclearage, the world was going to end at lunchtime, she tookoff her greenhat, put her busticket in her pocket and joined in the exercise.

The buspeople, and therewere many of them, were shockedand-surprised and amusedandannoyed, but when the word got around that the world was coming to an end at lunchtime, they put their pride in their pockets with their bustickets and madelove one with the other. And even the busconductor, being over, climbed into the cab and struck up some sort of relationship with the driver.

Thatnight, on the bus coming home, wewere all alittle embarrassed, especially me and the young lady in the greenhat, and we all started to say in different ways howhasty and foolish we had been. Butthen, always having been a bitofalad, i stood up and said it was a pity that the world didn't nearly end every lunchtime and that we could always pretend. And then it happened . . .

Quick asa crash we all changed partners and soon the bus was aquiver with white mothballbodies doing naughty things.

> And the next day
> And everyday
> In everybus
> In everystreet
> In everytown
> In everycountry

people pretended that the world was coming to an end at lunchtime. It still hasn't. Although in a way it has.

Roger McGough

repulsive: disgusting
nuclear age: age of nuclear weapons (hydrogen bombs, etc.)
being over: not having a partner
cab: driver's part of the bus
hasty: impulsive
a bit of a lad: rather a daring young man
aquiver: trembling
mothball bodies: mothballs are white balls of camphor which are put in clothes to keep moths away

Fire and ice

Some say the world will end in fire,
Some say in ice.
From what I've tasted of desire
I hold with those who favour fire.
But if it had to perish twice,
I think I know enough of hate
To say that for destruction ice
Is also great
And would suffice.

Robert Frost

perish: die
suffice: be enough

A prophecy

When pictures look alive with movements free,
When ships, like fishes, swim below the sea,
When men, outstripping birds, can span the sky,
Then half the world deep drenched in blood shall lie.

(Anonymous; written about AD 1400)

prophecy: prediction of the future
outstripping: going faster than
span: go right across
drenched: soaked

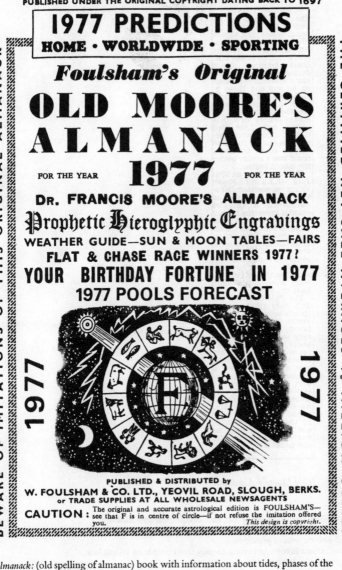

1697 — The Original Edition. — 1977

PUBLISHED UNDER THE ORIGINAL COPYRIGHT DATING BACK TO 1697

1977 PREDICTIONS
HOME · WORLDWIDE · SPORTING

Foulsham's Original

OLD MOORE'S ALMANACK 1977

FOR THE YEAR 1977 FOR THE YEAR

Dr. FRANCIS MOORE'S ALMANACK

Prophetic Hieroglyphic Engravings

WEATHER GUIDE—SUN & MOON TABLES—FAIRS

FLAT & CHASE RACE WINNERS 1977?

YOUR BIRTHDAY FORTUNE IN 1977

1977 POOLS FORECAST

PUBLISHED & DISTRIBUTED by

W. FOULSHAM & CO. LTD., YEOVIL ROAD, SLOUGH, BERKS.
or TRADE SUPPLIES AT ALL WHOLESALE NEWSAGENTS

CAUTION : The original and accurate astrological edition is FOULSHAM'S— see that F is in centre of circle—if not refuse the imitation offered you. *This design is copyright.*

(left margin) BEWARE OF IMITATIONS OF THIS ORIGINAL ALMANACK

(right margin) THE CERTIFIED NET SALE AVERAGES 1⅜ MILLION COPIES

almanack: (old spelling of almanac) book with information about tides, phases of the moon, anniversaries, etc.
flat & chase: two kinds of horse-race, flat and steeplechase (with jumps)
pools: football pools (system for gambling on the results of football matches)

Predictions for July

PREDICTIONS

The Full Moon on 1st July (3.26a.m.) sets opposition Mercury, square Pluto and sextile Uranus. An extremely violent configuration in the U.K. chart becomes exact during the month threatening murderous attacks on leaders and those in authority. This could mark a critical period for the government in maintaining credible power and Law and Order. Sino/Soviet border tensions are likely to become acute and India could lose a leader before the month begins.

The New Moon on 16th July (8.37a.m.) shows Venus opposition Neptune in square to the Ascendant. A call-girl scandal involving highly placed people could come to light. Financial frauds and the collapse of a large fashion company are indicated. The U.S.A. could be suddenly involved in a critical world confrontation possibly over the Middle East or Africa.

The Full Moon on the 30th July (10.54a.m.) is closely square to Uranus. Venus is in close conjunction with Jupiter. A very tense time for the world but in the U.K there could be concerted moves to defuse domestic tensions. There is a danger of severe transport disruptions and of serious rail and air crashes especially 22nd. At Goodwood the Stewards Cup my be won by the second favourite and favourites may be worth support in the non-handicaps.

(Old Moore's Almanack)

opposition Mercury, square Pluto, etc.: astrological terminology
Sino-Soviet: between China and the Soviet Union
call-girl: expensive prostitute
fraud: crime involving getting money from people by telling lies
defuse: make less explosive
Goodwood: racecourse for horses
Stewards Cup: a horse-race
non-handicaps: in handicap races, faster horses have to carry more weight

Your stars

By Diana
Britain's best-read astrologer

IS TODAY YOUR BIRTHDAY?
Your work attracts flattering attention. But it is your personality that draws people and a bit of money luck to you.

★ **LIBRA** (Sept 23-Oct 22): What you do and say makes an impact. Especially on top people and elderly relatives. One or two of them are in a generous mood. Love could produce a puzzle, and you may have one admirer too many.

☆ **SCORPIO** (Oct 23-Nov 22): You may think a friend, or lover, is disloyal. But he or she is probably worried, or under the weather. Your luck is better at work, where you are appreciated and make progress, and your colleagues or your boss think you're the tops.

★ **SAGITTARIUS** (Nov 23-Dec 20): You have a lot of friends today, yet you may feel a bit lonely. After midday an unexpected piece of business should cheer you up. Or you could meet someone you only know from work in a more friendly, personal fashion.

☆ **CAPRICORN** (Dec 21-Jan 19): Family business takes a turn for the better. You may not notice this at once, will quite soon. Look after and beauty, and don't to catch you out.

~~-Feb 18):

Which horoscope

[*Which?* is the magazine of the Consumers' Association. Among other things, it publishes the results of tests carried out on rival makes and brands of consumer goods, and recommends a 'best buy'. One month, *Which?* turned its attention to horoscopes.]

Most people will say there's nothing in horoscopes. So you would expect that most people wouldn't read them. But they do.

We thought we would try to find out how useful forecasts from stars really are, in their most accessible form – horoscopes in the press.

First of all we asked 1,000 people whether they read horoscopes, whether they found them useful, and what their reactions were.

Their reactions ranged from 'non-sense' and 'a load of rubbish' through 'they're fun' and 'amusing', to one person who always looked at them 'before making any major decision'.

To find out how good the advice and predictions really are, and see if there was any best buy, we asked some 200 people, some men, some women, some believers and some not, to read their horoscopes in the papers and magazines every day for a month, and to comment on them at the end of each day.

Rather sadly, 83 per cent reported that the advice was very little help at all. There wasn't much to choose between any of the newspapers and magazines we looked at but *Woman*, *Woman's Own* and the *Daily Mirror* were thought marginally less unhelpful than the average, while the *Sun* and the *News of the World* were thought worse.

Even if they are not very helpful,

horoscopes might at least be quite accurate. So we then asked our readers to say whether any predicted events actually happened.

Even worse: this time 87 per cent reported that predictions were not really very accurate at all.

Three magazines, *Woman*, *Woman's Own* and *Woman's Weekly*, were thought slightly less disastrously inaccurate than average, while the *Sunday Mirror* and once again the *Sun* and the *News of the World* were thought to be worse.

Before you read your horoscope you have to decide what sign you were born under. Unfortunately you may find that this depends on what newspaper you happen to be reading, as they could never all agree when one sign ended and the other began. The women's magazines, for example, could not even agree on the dates of Virgo. *Woman* and *Woman's Realm* thought it was from August 22 to September 22, *Woman's Own* from August 23 to September 22, and *Woman's Weekly* from August 24 to September 23. In fact, the dates of the signs change slightly from year to year. If you were born at the beginning or end of a sign, you'll have to go back to the records of the year you were born, and know the exact hour of your birth, to be sure which sign you do come under.

Having gone to the trouble to

discover your sign, just how significant is it? We checked this by sending predictions from the horoscopes to our helpers, and asking them how accurate they were. What we didn't tell them was that some of the predictions were for their own sign, and some were for completely different ones. Of course, if there was anything in them, predictions for their own sign should have been conspicuously more accurate.

Unfortunately the results proved otherwise. There was absolutely no difference in accuracy between reading your own horoscope and reading any other one.

(Extracts from a report in *Which?*)

accessible: easy to get hold of
marginally: slightly
sign: sign of the zodiac, related to the sun's position in the sky at different times of the year
conspicuously: very clearly

*"But Mars is in conjunction with Saturn, and I'm a Capricorn!
I wasn't supposed to be knocked down by a car today!"*

(Punch)

Monday's child is... fair of face,
Tuesday's child is full of grace,
Wednesday's child is full of woe,
Thursday's child has far to go,
Friday's child is loving and giving,
Saturday's child works hard for a living,
But the child that is born on the Sabbath Day
Is happy and wise and good and gay

(Traditional rhyme)

THURSDAY'S CHILD
HAS FAR TO GO

Thursday people are natural extroverts with a taste for the best in life. This is hardly surprising when you realise they're ruled by the luxury-loving planet Jupiter.

Those born under Jupiter's auspices usually have their fair share of success, and in most cases they have achieved this by their own go-getting. Jupiter is also one of the planets that rules travel, so Thursday's children have far to go, literally, in their taste for adventure, as well as in pursuit of their ambitions.

Their colour is blue, the colour of the sea and sky, preferably an azure or dark blue. Their gems, too, are blue, such as sapphires, and they should aim to look well groomed rather than fussy or frilly.

Thursday people should try to find interesting jobs which are not entirely routine, or at the very least an interesting hobby.

(*Woman*)

Sabbath: Sunday
extroverts: lively, outgoing people
auspices: protection
go-getting: energetic, dynamic behaviour
azure: bright blue
gems: jewels
well groomed: carefully dressed
fussy, frilly: wearing clothes with lots of ornamentation

(*Time Out*)

tarot: fortune-telling with a special kind of cards
clairvoyant: person who can see what is happening at a distance
chirologist: hand-reader

ULTIMATE IN STRIKES!
Ghost causes 'walk outs'

A GHOST who works non-union hours at a Birmingham car plant has even caused strikes, says the city's "Evening Mail."

Added credence to the apparition's activities comes from a security officer at Leyland's Perry Barr plant.

Jack Denson saw a spirit figure dressed in a grey suit. "I felt the blood drain from me and could not move for a while," he says. "Then I ran."

The paper takes the amusing angle that the ghost "works overtime. The factory phantom has already upset employees and even caused a few 'walk outs.'

"Providing he keeps his distance and doesn't apply for union membership, neither the management nor the men mind him setting up his haunting business at Leyland's plant."

Frank Davies, manager of an axle division, says the ghost has frightened "a few of his men over the years." Those who had not seen the figure regarded it as "a bit of a joke."

During the drought, an old well was discovered at the plant. Some years ago a man fell down it and was killed.

"The well was sealed and that was the end of the matter until we started uncovering it," says Davies.

Foreman Cliff Brown saw the form about two months ago. "Something made me turn. I saw this grey figure. My hair stood on end. Then 'it' disappeared."

(*Psychic News*)

credence: (support for) belief
angle: attitude
overtime: extra hours
phantom: ghost
haunting: word used to refer to the activity of ghosts
axle: part of a car which the wheel turns on
drought: long dry period
sealed: closed up

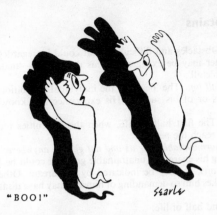

"BOO!"   Searle

Love is an inside-out nightie

GIRLS! Here's a great way to find out the name of your future husband.

According to an old superstition, you will dream of your husband-to-be if you—

Wear your nightie inside out.

OR sleep with a mirror under your pillow.

OR count nine stars each night, for nine nights.

OR rub your bedposts with a lemon.

OR eat 100 chicken gizzards.

OR fill your mouth with water and run three times round the houses.

The first man you see as you run will have the same name as your future spouse.

If you don't believe me, ask researcher Alvin Schwartz.

He's about to publish a book called Cross Your Fingers, Spit In Your Hat—a collection of the superstitions and odd customs people use to help them through life.

And he has found that we're just as anxious to court Lady Luck as any other generation.

We don't just believe old wives' tales — we're busy making up new ones

Mr Schwartz says: " We rely on superstitions for the same reasons people always have.

" When we are faced with situations we cannot control—which depend on luck or chance—superstitions make us feel more secure."

(John Hill, *Sun*)

---

nightie: night-dress
gizzard: part of a bird's digestive system
spouse: marriage partner

superstition: belief in luck, magic, etc.
court: try to get the favour of
old wives' tales: superstitions

Dreaming of mountains

MOUNTAINS (Hills) Obstacles and difficulties that could be regarded as a challenge. The dreamer may be exaggerating his difficulties – 'making a mountain out of a molehill'.

The mountain-top or hill-top: The 'peak' of the individual's ambitions, the 'height' of his powers or of his success. His experience and knowledge. The goal.

Climbing mountains: The first half of life, when the difficulties must be overcome in order to reach the peak.

Struggling to scale insurmountable heights and not getting anywhere:
The dreamer is wasting his energy on unattainable goals; it could be better spent in other directions, as may be indicated by the dream. Otherwise this conceit, which makes him so demanding of himself, may have disastrous consequences.

Descending: The second half of life.

Parts of the body.
Mountain ledge: The bosom.
Being in the valley between high mountains: Protection, security, comfort, which can easily turn to isolation and imprisonment.

(Tom Chetwynd, *Dictionary for Dreamers*)

scale: climb
insurmountable: unclimbable
conceit: high opinion of oneself
bosom: breasts

gill: dialect word for a mountain stream cut deep into the ground
2150 feet: 1,000 feet is about 300 metres
fell: dialect word for a mountain
confluence: meeting point of two streams
contouring: following contour lines, keeping at the same level
heather: mountain plant
crag: rock wall
tortuous: twisting
slabby: slabs are flat stones
intimidating: frightening
facade: wall
scree: steep slope of loose stone
ravine: cutting made by a stream
bilberry: small fruit found on bushes on mountain-sides
gully: same as *ravine*
pinnacle: spike of rock
arete: sharp ridge
scrambling: between walking and climbing

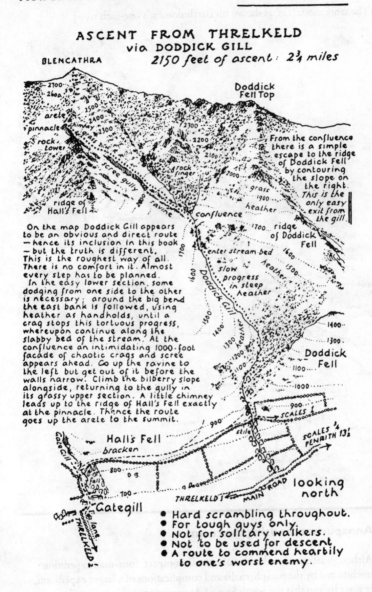

ASCENT FROM THRELKELD
via DODDICK GILL
2150 feet of ascent : 2¼ miles

BLENCATHRA

2700
2600
arête
pinnacle
chimney
2500
2300
rock
tower
2300
scree gully
ravine
ridge of
Hall's Fell

Doddick
Fell Top

2300
1200
2100
rock
finger
2000

From the confluence
there is a simple
escape to the ridge
of Doddick Fell
by contouring
the slope on
the right.
This is the
only easy
exit from
the gill.

grass
1900
heather
confluence
1700 ridge
of Doddick
Fell

enter stream bed
1600
slow
progress
in steep
heather

1500
heather

On the map Doddick Gill appears
to be an obvious and direct route
— hence its inclusion in this book
— but the truth is different.
This is the roughest way of all.
There is no comfort in it. Almost
every step has to be planned.
In the easy lower section, some
dodging from one side to the other
is necessary ; around the big bend
the east bank is followed, using
heather as handholds, until a
crag stops this tortuous progress,
whereupon continue along the
slabby bed of the stream. At the
confluence an intimidating 1000-foot
facade of chaotic crags and scree
appears ahead. Go up the ravine to
the left but get out of it before the
walls narrow. Climb the bilberry slope
alongside, returning to the gully in
its grassy upper section. A little chimney
leads up to the ridge of Hall's Fell exactly
at the pinnacle. Thence the route
goes up the arête to the summit.

1700
1600
Doddick Gill
1500
1400
1300 heather
1200 heather
1100

1400
1300

Doddick
Fell

1100
1000
900
SCALES
stile
900
SCALES ¼
PENRITH 13½

Hall's Fell
bracken

800   O.S.
fell
700

Gategill

THRELKELD MAIN ROAD

looking
north

Gate Gill
fell
lane
THRELKELD

THRELKELD ↑

- Hard scrambling throughout.
- For tough guys only.
- Not for solitary walkers.
- Not to be used for descent.
- A route to commend heartily
  to one's worst enemy.

(A. Wainwright, *A Pictorial Guide to the Lakeland Fells*)

Blencathra again

[The same mountain, as shown on Bartholomew's one-inch map]

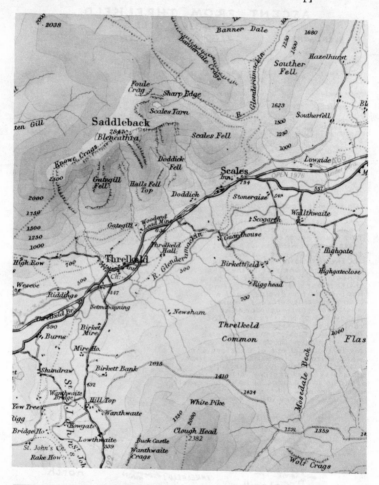

Annapurna: choosing the team

Although attracted to the idea of a small, compact, four-man expedition uncluttered by the paraphernalia and complications of a larger expedition, it was obvious that the South Face of Annapurna would require a larger party. Six men also seemed insufficient and we went up to eight.

The next problem was the selection of the team from the numerous leading climbers of Britain. They would have to be the men who could climb at a very high standard on rock and ice, with plenty of endurance, and an ability to subordinate their own personal ambitions to the good of the expedition as a whole. Most important of all, they would have to get on together. Many top-class climbers, having a touch of the prima donna in their make-up, are often self-centred and are essentially individualists; in some ways the best expedition man is the steady plodder. On the South Face of Annapurna we were going to need a high proportion of hard lead climbers who would be able to take over the exacting front position as others slowed up and tired.

One can never be sure of anyone's individual performance in the Himalayas, since people acclimatise to altitude at different rates and some never acclimatise at all. The safest bet, therefore, is to take out climbers who have already proved themselves at altitude, but because of the ban on climbing in Nepal and Pakistan in the late sixties, there was a distinct shortage of top-standard Alpinists with Himalayan experience.

I approached Ian Clough first. I had done some of my best climbing with him and quite apart from being a capable mountaineer he was also the kindest and least selfish partner I had known. Certainly the perfect expedition man, he had very little personal ambition, but was always ready to do his best for the project as a whole.

Then I asked twenty-eight-year-old Mick Burke and, thirdly, Don Whillans. In some ways, Don was the most obvious choice of all, yet the one about whom I had the most doubts. Although certainly the finest all-round mountaineer that Britain had produced since the war, in the previous years he had allowed himself to slip into poor physical condition. He had lost interest in British rock-climbing, and even the Alps, preferring to go on expeditions to the farther ranges of the world. In spite of a strained relationship, which was ever-present, I had done some of my best climbing with him, each of us irritating the other, yet at the same time complementing each other's weak points.

(Chris Bonington, *The Next Horizon*)

uncluttered: not weighed down
paraphernalia: large variety of equipment
Annapurna: very high mountain in the Himalayas
endurance: ability to keep going for a long time
prima donna: person who is proud, temperamental and difficult to manage (literally, chief woman singer in an opera)
plodder: steady, unimaginative person
exacting: difficult, demanding
acclimatise to altitude: get used to height
ban: prohibition (climbing was forbidden)
complementing: providing what was lacking

Annapurna: success

I opened up the radio at five o'clock and Dougal came on.

'Hello, Dougal, this is Chris at IV. Did you manage to get out of the tent today?'

'Aye, we've got some good news for you. We reached the top.'

Don told me the story the following day. They had reached the top of the fixed ropes but unable to find a suitable place for a camp site they plodded on up through the soft snow on the ridge. They had not bothered to put the rope on, and were not using oxygen, finding that in spite of the very strong wind, the climbing was quite easy. It was twelve o'clock before they found a suitable site for Camp VII but by then they were just below the final headwall of the ridge and the summit seemed very close. As there was no point in having a top camp so high, they just kept plodding.

The climbing became more difficult, up steep snow-covered rocks, the last fifty feet vertical with big flat holds. Don said:

'Generally, I had done hardly any leading at all up to this point, but I felt completely confident, and it never occurred to me to use the rope.'

Once over the top of the ridge the wind immediately dropped and they found that the north side of the mountain was quite warm and pleasant with sun breaking through clouds. While waiting for Dougal to follow, Don looked around for the anchor point for the rope they would need to get back down.

The summit itself was a real knife-edge and there was not much to see from the top. The northern slope dropped away into the cloud, a great boulder field part-concealed by snow. The only tops visible were the other two summits of Annapurna; everything else, including the entire South Face, was blanketed in cloud.

Don said: 'We stayed there for about ten minutes. At this stage we didn't feel much in the way of elation – it was difficult to believe it was all over and anyway we still had to get back down.'

(Chris Bonington, *The Next Horizon*)

IV: camp four
aye: yes
plodded: walked on slowly and steadily
site: place
anchor point: place to fix the rope
elation: great happiness

The rising cost of buying up a top mountain

In this imaginary interview with Cassius Bonehead, the well-known climber Ian McNaught-Davis satirizes the commercialism of modern mountaineering.

McNAUGHT: How did it all start, Cass?

CASSIUS: Well, you see, Mac, I wanted to lead an expedition to the hardest small peak in the world. A new trial to test my developing personality.

Mac.: You'd need a strong team for that.

Cass.: Yes. I chose three of my very closest friends and we formed the hardest team of climbers in the world.

Mac.: Sounds good.

Cass.: Ah. That's when the problems start. Low peak – low box office. Nobody buys lousy routes on small peaks. We really needed a bigger scene. That's when I thought about Annaplus, the biggest and hardest face in the world.

Mac.: But that would cost real money.

Cass.: We estimated about £500,000 including oxygen and larks' tongues for the porters. A hundred thousand of rope and twenty thousand man days of margarine.

Mac.: A hundred thousand feet, that's impressive.

Cass.: Yards, old boy, yards.

Mac.: Where did you get the cash?

Cass.: Nobody is interested in cheap, trashy peaks. Annaplus isn't the highest but its face is the hardest in the world and by the time we were finished we believed it was the highest. You see it's a marketing problem, old boy. In the professional climbing world we call it creative mountaineering marketing. You find the mountain, create the image, sell like hell and then go out and climb it. If you get all this right, money falls on you like snow on the north face

of Annaplus. We created the hardest route in the world on Annaplus, and who can resist that.

Mac.: But it would take more than four of you?

Cass.: Yes, that was a problem. In fact we ended up with 86.

Mac.: That includes the porters?

Cass.: No. There were 16,000 of them, in fact the whole of the working population of the country. We had 10 cameramen, four announcers, six producers, eight sound men, six lighting specialists, four make-up specialists, six camp managers, one for each camp, my English, American and European agents and 41 climbers and a partridge in a pear tree.

Mac.: That seems quite a change from four close friends.

Cass.: Yes I agree, but we were the hardest group of climbers ever to leave Britain, in fact none were left. They were all close loyal friends. We did have one American who's the hardest climber in the States and also the most religious. The idea came from my agent and it guaranteed the American sales of my book and implicitly got God into the team at the same time.

Mac.: I'm impressed, Cass. How did the climb go.

Cass.: We were fantastically successful. It took nine months to climb the first 500 feet. Harder than the North face of the Eiger. Then two of the hardest men pushed through the next 8,000 feet to the summit. Artificial climbing all the way on overhanging ice with constant avalanches. It took them nearly all day. On the summit their anoraks were whipped by 200 mile an hour winds as they ate their margarine sandwiches.

Mac.: What's next? Anything must seem dull after your last tremendous achievement.

Cass.: This year's hardest climb in the world is the South face of Everest. Great box office. An international team from 90 countries, 200 climbers. It's the Grand Slam. They are going to climb it by every route and they've got world wide rights for film, books and this time it's covered by the BBC not crummy old ITV who didn't like to move out of base camp. It's fantastic.

Mac.: Are you going, Cass.?

Cass.: I was asked but I decided not to go. You see, old man, the whole thing is getting a bit too commercialised for me.

(The Observer)

low box office: we wouldn't make much money out of it (the box office is the ticket office of a cinema or theatre)
lousy: (slang) worthless
larks' tongues: a very expensive food (a lark is a kind of bird)
trashy: rubbishy
a partridge in a pear tree: joking reference to the Christmas carol 'The Twelve Days of Christmas' ('On the twelfth day of Christmas my true love gave to me twelve drummers drumming, eleven pipers piping, . . . two turtle doves and a partridge in a pear tree')
implicitly: without saying so directly

Is Everest growing taller?

An unconsidered hazard awaits the 1975 British Everest Expedition led by Chris Bonington, who will be arriving in Kathmandu this morning. The top of Mount Everest is moving, probably upwards and possibly at an astonishingly rapid rate. Nobody, in any case, knows quite how high Everest really is.

Attention was focused on this problem by the announcement from Peking Radio that Chinese surveyors and geologists had completed a new measurement of the peak, and found that it was 29,029.24 feet high—more than a foot higher than the figure usually accepted in the west.

Opinion among British climbers about the height of the mountain reflects the scientists' uncertainty. Christopher Brasher, writing in *The Observer* this weekend, claimed that Everest stuck its summit to a height of 29,145 feet. This is actually an estimate four feet higher than one made in 1905 for the mountain's height above the spheroid, an outdated way of measuring mountains even

then. The height above the geoid, the mathematical level taken as the basis of modern readings, was only 29,032 feet.

Dougal Haston, who is now on his third expedition to Everest, optimistically supposed before setting out that the mountain was a mere 29,002 feet. This notion is based on data even more antiquated than Brasher's. Brigadier Gardiner says that the first measurements of Everest, in the nineteenth century, gave the height as 29,000 feet. The surveyors added two feet to give their figure a semblance of accuracy.

The Survey of India took fresh measurements in the years 1952 to 1954. The scatter of results from different stations have heights up to 16 feet apart, but the accepted average which became the official Western figure was 29,028 feet.

Nick Estcourt, another member of the expedition, who is a civil engineer by training, things the Chinese may have made the mountain higher themselves before measuring it. " At least one Chinese expedition has climbed the mountain from their side, and they left behind a bust of Chairman Mao. Perhaps that is a foot high. Anyway, if the mountain is bobbing up and down, we must just hope to catch it on a low day."

(*The Times*)

---

hazard: problem, danger
focused: directed
29,029.24 feet: 8,848 metres
a foot: about 30 cm
spheroid: almost exactly spherical body
geoid: body (not an exact sphere) the same shape as the earth would be if its surface was levelled
semblance: appearance

Mountaineering.— Guides.

Voyage dans les Montagnes.—Guides.

1 We have reached the summit.

Nous voici arrivés au sommet.

2 Which way must I descend from the summit ?

De quel côté dois-je descendre du sommet ?

3 We had better be roped on the way down.

Il vaut mieux descendre à l'aide de la corde.

4 We have descended too low.

Nous sommes descendus trop bas.

5 We had better wait until the mist has scattered a little.

Nous ferions mieux d'attendre que le brouillard se fût un peu dissipé.

6 All traces of the path have disappeared.

Les traces du sentier sont effacées.

7 How shall I recover the path ?

Comment pourrai-je retrouver le sentier ?

8 It is my belief that you have lost your way.

Il me semble que vous avez perdu votre chemin.

9 Tell me the honest truth — have you ever been this way before ?

Dites-moi la vérité— avez-vous déjà été ici ?

10 How deep is the abyss ?

Quelle est la profondeur de l'abime—du précipice ?

(*Murray's Handbook of Travel-Talk*, published 1897)

summit: top of a mountain
abyss: very deep hole or precipice

THE TIMES turns its attention to cats

25 years ago

From The Times of Thursday, September 7, 1950

Matterhorn climber

From Our Correspondent

Geneva, Sept 6.—A new conquest of the Matterhorn, this time by a 10-month-old black and white kitten, is reported from the Hotel Belvedere (10,820ft), on the Hörnli Ridge—the starting point for alpinists attempting to climb the mountain.

The kitten, accustomed to watch from his hotel home the dawn departure of climbers, decided one morning to follow in their footsteps.

[Two mornings later] he was seen by a group of climbers, who passed him by, convinced that his climbing skill, if not his spirit, would be defeated. . . . They were wrong, and hours later the cat, meowing and tail up, reached the summit (14,780ft), where the incredulous climbing party rewarded him with a share of their meal.

Kitten on the Matterhorn

From Mr C. R. Simpson

Sir, Your reprint today (September 8) from "25 years ago" certainly revived the memory of one who was there. The kitten, which was in fact four months old, not ten months, climbed the Matterhorn on August 18 and 19, 1950, and was carried down by an Italian guide to the Riondet Hut in Italy.

On August 21, Alfred Biner, a Zermatt guide, and I traversed the Matterhorn, descending into Italy. We returned over the Furggjoch, bringing the triumphant kitten back to Zermatt, whence it eventually reached its home at the Hotel Belvedere.

Yours faithfully,
CHRISTOPHER R. SIMPSON,
The Clock House,
Roman Road,
Birstall, Leicester.

The Matterhorn: alpine mountain, also called *Mont Cervin*
incredulous: unable to believe what they saw

Cats studied as clues to human migrations

From Winston Groom
Washington, Sept 29

For 15 years, Dr Neil Todd has been searching for cats. Not big cats, like lions or tigers or pumas or leopards; nor fancy cats, like overbred Persians or Abyssinians or Siamese or Angoras.

What interests him are alley cats. And in pursuit of these animals, Dr Todd has beaten a 20-nation trail of cat-spotting from the back alleys of Chicago to the bazaars of Istanbul, from the frozen wastes of Iceland to the heat of Sudan.

"There are a lot of mysteries that can be solved with cats", he says. "If we can understand cats, we can understand a lot more about ourselves."

Dr Todd, a professor of biology at Boston University, is involved in a grand scheme to prepare maps of the world's cat populations.

Recently he led teams of cat spotters into the cities and villages of Iran and Greece to spot as many cats as they can, examine them closely if possible and log their characteristics for his great cat map—which, when completed, will look something like a global weather chart.

Dr Todd's fascination with the cat stems in part from his conviction that when enough profiles of its genetic mutations are compiled, they will shed light on past human migrations, trade and commercial routes.

The cat was there long before man came on the scene. Fossil records dating back 40 million years show that the cat abounded in remarkably smilar form to his modern successor. Then in time it developed into two distinct strains—greater and lesser cats.

(The Times)

Zoologists have divided living cats into two groups, based in part on the noise they make.

Large cats, of the genus *Panthera*, are unable to purr because of a peculiar development of a bone between their tongue and larynx. Instead, these cats roar. The other group, called *Felis*, includes most domestic cats.

"My own persistent interest", Dr Todd says, "is that there is a problem to be solved. The domestication of the cat and its dispersion comes closest to the parallel of the urbanization of man. It shows us something of early humans."

overbred: too far removed from the natural state
alley cats: ordinary cats (an alley is a back street)
spotting: looking for
log: write down, record
global: world-wide
stems: originates
mutations: changes
abounded: was very common
strains: types
purr: the noise a cat makes when it's happy
dispersion: scattering
urbanization: adapting to city life

Cat smell dispute makes 600 men idle

By R. W. Shakespeare
Northern Industrial Correspondent

While the attention of Parliament and much of the nation was focused on the struggle for survival in Britain's car industry, and the multi-million-pound cost of trying to save the jobs of thousands of workers, about six hundred men from the Leyland Triumph car plant at Speke, Liverpool, were idle yesterday because of an unofficial strike by 21 workers who complained of a smell caused bv stray cats.

The 21 men in the trim shop walked out on Monday, complaining about dirt and smell caused by the cats. Work stopped while cleaners spent 45 minutes scrubbing the floor. Then the men protested that the floor was still wet and dangerous to work on.

They decided to hold a meeting, having been warned by the management that if they did so they would not be paid for the time lost. Earlier the management had agreed with shop stewards that payment should be made for the time when the workshop was being cleaned.

At the meeting the 21 workers decided to strike as a protest against the management's refusal to pay them. Yesterday they were still out and the 600 other workers were laid off.

Production in the trim shop was stopped, although assembly of the TR7 sports car, one of the best-selling export models, was continuing, using trim components from stock. If stocks run out before the strike ends, car production may be halted

(The Times)

---

idle: out of work
stray: homeless
trim shop: part of the factory which makes the trim (= decorative metal strips) for cars
laid off: sent away from work
assembly: putting together

Fog

The fog comes
On little cat feet.
It sits looking
Over harbor and city
On silent haunches
And then moves on.

Carl Sandburg

---

haunches: place where the legs join the body

141

A hurricane

The wind by now was more than redoubled. The shutters were bulging as if tired elephants were leaning against them, and Father was trying to tie the fastening with that handkerchief. But to push against this wind was like pushing against rock. The handkerchief, shutters, everything burst: the rain poured in like the sea into a sinking ship, the wind occupied the room, snatching pictures from the wall, sweeping the table bare. Through the gaping frames the lightning-lit scene without was visible. The creepers, which before had looked like cobwebs, now streamed up into the sky like new-combed hair. Bushes were lying flat, laid back on the ground as close as a rabbit lays back his ears. Branches were leaping about loose in the sky. The negro huts were clean gone, and the negroes crawling on their stomachs across the compound to gain the shelter of the house. The bouncing rain seemed to cover the ground with a white smoke, a sort of sea in which they wallowed like porpoises. One boy began to roll away: his mother, forgetting caution, rose to her feet: and immediately the fat old woman was blown right away, bowling along across fields and hedgerows like someone in a funny fairy-story, till she landed up against a wall and was pinned there, unable to move. But the others managed to reach the house, and soon could be heard in the cellar underneath.

Moreover the very floor began to ripple, as a loose carpet will ripple on a gusty day: in opening the cellar door the negroes had let the wind in, and now for some time they could not shut it again. The wind, to push against, was more like a solid block than a current of air.

(Richard Hughes, *A High Wind in Jamaica*)

shutters: pieces of wood fixed over the windows
bulging: curving inwards under the pressure
gaping: wide open
without: outside
creepers: plants which grow on walls
cobwebs: the silk constructions made by spiders
wallowed: moved heavily up and down
porpoises: sea-animals
bowling: turning over and over
pinned: trapped
ripple: move like waves

When the Thames froze solid

The Thames has often been locked in winter's icy grip. In centuries past, when its bed was much wider, ice would form at the sides, and as the frost increased, would extend from bank to bank.

In 1434 it was frozen over below London Bridge, as far down as Gravesend, and the frost lasted from November 24 till February 10.

In 1515 the ice on the river was strong enough to bear carriages and many passed over between Lambeth and Westminster. The first frost fair occurred in 1564 and the one in 1608 caused great gaiety. Bowling and dancing occurred between Lambeth and Westminster and booths selling beer, wine and shoes soon appeared. There was even a barber's shop.

The most celebrated frost fair was in 1684. The Thames was frozen and on January 1 streets of booths were set upon the Thames. On the sixth the river was frozen over and soon coaches and carts crossed from the North to the South bank.

As the frost grew more severe, the Thames beyond London was planted with booths in formal streets. All sorts of shops prospered, including a printing press, where ladies liked to have their names printed, and the day and the year when they walked on the Thames. The printer made his fortune and nightly prayed for the severe weather to continue. One fine day and his thriving new business would sink without trace.

Coaches plied from Westminster and to the Temple. Soon the Thames surface resembled a carnival and the attractions included skating, bull-bating, horse and coach races and puppet plays. The thaw set in on February 5 and the booths were speedily removed. King Charles II accompanied by members of the Royal household made many visits to the festivities.

(*South Kensington News and Chelsea Post*)

bowling: game played by rolling large balls
booths: temporary shops
prospered: did well
thriving: prospering
plied: carried passengers
bull-baiting: old sport which involved sending bulldogs to attack a bull
puppet: kind of doll used for theatrical shows
thaw: warm weather when the snow and ice melt

Same old scenes in the snow

The first heavy snow of the year took the South of England by surprise as usual yesterday. The snowdrifts at Brighton station caused as much consternation as if they had suddenly appeared in the Sahara.

The stationmaster rose to the occasion at 2 a.m. by walking four miles from his home to organise digging operations. But the faster the team of 30 men dug, the faster the snowflakes came down. By the time the commuters were ready to leave for their London offices, the trains were still trapped in the sidings by drifts seven feet high.

Southern Region services were disorganised all the way to London. With the big hold-up at Brighton and those now familiar hazards of 'icing on the conductor rails' and on the running rails, it was inevitable that many were four hours late for

work and others did not get there at all.

Passengers at Brighton listened to a bleak announcement over the station loudspeaker at 9 a.m. 'We have no information of trains to London. Conditions are very serious. Unless it is really necessary, passengers are advised not to travel.'

One innocent recently returned from a Mediterranean climate thought how pretty the three inches of snow looked at 7·30 a.m. in Crowborough, Sussex, and was astonished to find himself regarded as slightly unreasonable because he tried to catch a train at the local station shortly before nine.

'Everyone else has given it up and gone away,' they told him. 'We did have a train through about 7 a.m. but we aren't expecting any more.' Finally, he put chains on his car, drove to Tonbridge station and arrived in London by a series of local trains just in time for lunch.

(*Guardian*)

snowdrifts: places where the snow is deep
consternation: great surprise
commuters: people who travel into town daily to work
sidings: places where trains are kept when they are not running
conductor rails: rails that carry the electric current
bleak: cold, comfortless

Oxford–London train timetable

Oxford → Didcot → Reading → London
Mondays to Fridays

	Oxford depart	Didcot depart	Reading arrive	Reading depart	Heathrow arrive ▲ 🚌	Paddington arrive
🐛	01 07X	→	01 44X			
				02 30M	→	03 10M
		04 02X	04 25X	04 30X	06 45	05 20X
		04 12M	04 35M	04 40M	06 45	05 30M
		05 37	06 00	06 10	07 30	06 50
				06 17	→	07 12
				06 37	→	07 32
🐛	06 03	06 25	06 56	06 57	08 30	07 48
🐛				07 07	→	08 00
🐛	06 35	06 51	07 22	07 22	09 00	08 06
				07 25	→	08 02
				07 34	→	08 09
🐛	07 00	07 16	07 46	07 48	09 30	08 23
🐛	07 00	07 28	→	→	→	08 12
🐛	07 20	→	07 52	07 54	09 30	08 29
🐛				08 02	→	08 39
		07 38	08 05	08 05	09 30	08 44
◻ 🐛	07 40	07 54	08 12	08 12	09 30	08 47
🐛		08 02	→	→	→	08 53
🐛				08 22	→	08 58
🐛				08 32	→	09 12
		08 06	08 36	08 37	10 00	09 27
	07 52	08 16	08 50	08 52	10 30	09 38
◻ 🐛	08 10	08 24	→	→	→	09 15
◻ 🐛				09 04	→	09 42
◻		08 47	09 08	09 08	10 30	09 50
				09 14	→	09 50
				09 17	→	10 09
🐛	08 32	08 55	09 26	09 29	11 00	10 23
◻		09 09	→	→	→	09 53
✕ ◻ 🐛	09 03	→	→	→	→	10 05
	09 10	09 25	09 47	09 47	11 30	10 30

🚌 Change at Reading for Railair Link coach service direct to Heathrow Airport ▲

Times in heavy type (e.g. **07 30**) represent through services; those in light type (e.g. 20 00) indicate connecting services and passengers are advised to enquire where to change trains.

Notes
🐛 Does not operate Holiday Mondays 3 January, 11 April
d Departs
p Previous night
A Until 27 February
B From 6 March
M Mondays only
S Stops to set down only
U Stops to pick up passengers only
X Except Mondays
▲ A revised Railair service operates on 3 January, 8 and 11 April, please check before travelling

For whole or part of journey
✕ Restaurant service according to time of day
◻ Drinks and cold snacks
ⓘ Hot dishes to order, also buffet service

"I don't normally get this one I'm usually on the 8.48 that stops at Wiggleswick Purley and Black Heath but this morning I overslept because I was so late getting back on the so-called 19.49 non-stop train due to leave at 20.15 anyway it turned out they'd cancelled it because of a points failure at Kershaw Green so I ended up having to change at Poulsden Park this is normally a good one to get it gets you in to London Bridge at 10.41 but today because they've closed the tunnel at Maudling (South) to do repair work we'll have to change at Corbett Woodall and get on the 11.07 which is coming up from Bournemouth due into Waterloo at 12.14 she's usually on time so we'll have to look sharpish as I don't expect they'll wait for connecting passengers failing that there won't be another one through till 12.05 and that's a stopper. . . "

(*Private Eye Book of Bores*)

points: place where two railway lines divide
look sharpish: (slang) hurry

The longest-named railway station in the world is in North Wales. It is:

LLANFAIRPWLLGWYNGYLLGOGERYCHWYRNDROBWLL-LLANTYSILIOGOGOGOCH.

(The station's nameplate, by the way, is 26 yards long.)

26 yards: about 24 metres

> ## BEWARE OF TRAINS
> ## GOING BOTH WAYS
> ## AT ONCE

(Notice at Durham level crossing)

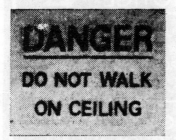

This sign, incorporating an appropriate warning as we start the office party season, was photographed in a London museum by Marian Campbell of St John's Wood.

(*The Times*)

There was a young man from Darjeeling
Who got on a bus going to Ealing.
It said on the door
'Don't spit on the floor'
So he lay down and spat on the ceiling.

NOTICES

GREATER LONDON COUNCIL
DOGS PROHIBITED

LONDON COUNTY COUNCIL
NOTICE
HAWKERS, TRADERS, & OTHERS,
ARE PROHIBITED FROM CALLING,
SHOUTING, OR USING ANY BELL,
OR OTHER INSTRUMENT IN
THESE BUILDINGS. *BY ORDER*

NOTICE
PASSENGERS MUST NOT ATTEMPT TO
ENTER OR LEAVE CARS BEYOND THIS
POINT, NOR CROSS THE LINE EXCEPT
BY THE BRIDGE OR SUBWAY PROVIDED.

WARNING TO STAFF
DO NOT STEP ON ANY RAIL

PRIVATE YARD
There is a Public Footpath
up this Yard, but it is
NOT A THOROUGHFARE
FOR VEHICLES.

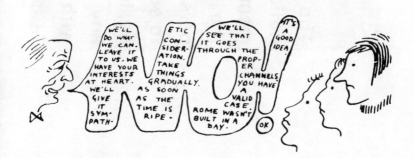

REWARD

The London Clearing Banks will, until further notice, pay a reward of up to £5,000 to any member of the public who gives information to the Police leading to the conviction of any person for stealing or attempting or conspiring to steal any of their property, wherever it may be, in the United Kingdom, or for breaking into any of their branches in the United Kingdom with intent to steal.

SEPTEMBER 1977

Police questioning, arrest and bail:

Before arrest:
The police cannot detain you to ask questions without first arresting you. If you are driving a motor vehicle, you must give your name, address and age if required.

You do not have to 'accompany the police to the station' or 'help the police with their enquiries' unless you want to or unless you have been arrested.

On arrest:
If you are arrested, the police must tell you what you are charged with. They should caution you — tell you of your right not to say anything.

You should be allowed to telephone your family, a friend or a solicitor, and be allowed to talk to your solicitor in private.

You do not have to answer questions. If you do, make sure a record is kept of both questions and answers in full and only sign it if it is correct. Also, make your own record at the time or as soon as possible afterwards. If you are in any doubt, do not say anything until you have taken legal advice. If you do make a statement it is often better to write it yourself. Only sign it if it is correct.

Any property taken from you must be listed and the list signed as correct by you.

The police have no right to fingerprint you unless you agree or they have a magistrate's order to do so. Except for blood, urine and breath tests for driving offences, you cannot be physically examined or tested unless you agree. If you do, you have the right to have a doctor, lawyer or friend present.

You cannot be compelled to take part in an identification parade. **It may be to your advantage to do so but take legal advice first.**

Do not make any deals with the police, such as agreeing to plead guilty in return for bail, or admitting to a minor offence in return for not being charged with a more serious one. Such deals are unlikely to help and will probably lessen your chances of acquittal.

Bail:
Bail means releasing an arrested person until the trial. Refusal of bail results in going to prison or a remand centre for up to 8 days.

Ask for bail. The police have the power to grant bail at the police station. They must do so unless the offence is very serious, or they bring you before a magistrate within 24 hours, or you have been arrested on a warrant which does not allow bail.

If you are refused bail, call a solicitor, or get a friend to do so, and tell him when and where you will be appearing in court. Give him the names and addresses of possible sureties — friends or relatives who will pledge a sum of money to the police or the court should you fail to attend your trial.

In court:
Get legal advice and assistance from a solicitor.
If you appear in court without a solicitor, ask for a remand (an adjournment until you can get advice), ask for bail, and ask for legal aid.

(Information provided by National Council for Civil Liberties)

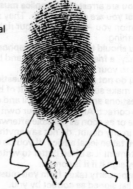

(*The Big Red Diary*)

detain: hold
acquittal: being declared innocent
remand centre: place where people are held before trial
warrant: arrest document signed by a magistrate
adjournment: postponement, delay

A policeman talks about his work

PHILIP: The job isn't at all dangerous provided you use a lot of common sense and don't try too much of a tough approach. I find that tact and good humour is a much better weapon than a physical assault. For instance, if I see a fight, the first thing I do is to try and assess the situation. If it's a big fight, I stand back and radio for assistance (we carry small radios), but if there's just two people fighting – usually because they are drunk – I step in and most of the time the uniform has the effect of separating them and, although they might continue to argue, we can usually come to a British compromise.

INTERVIEWER: What else do you do as a policeman?

PHILIP: I walk the streets helping people, arresting those who do wrong, advising motorists and reporting them if they transgress our traffic laws. We also deal with a lot of thefts and house burglaries, very seldom with fights involving knives or guns. I've only been shot at once in my service – and he missed! We're supposed to wear a wooden truncheon but I don't because we wear it in an inside pocket and it pulls my trousers down!

INTERVIEWER: Do you think some policemen would like to carry guns?

PHILIP: No thank you, we don't want them. A lot of robberies are committed with arms now anyway but if we were armed, even more would be committed with guns. I'm totally opposed to carrying guns.

assess the situation: decide exactly what is happening
transgress: break
truncheon: policeman's club

A free country

The British consciousness of civil liberty can perhaps be best encapsulated in the two popular assertions, 'It's a free country', and 'I know my rights'. It is of great value that this consciousness runs so deep, but it is very fuzzy, perhaps because our liberties are so imprecise. Nowhere are they defined in a constitution, though lawyers will claim they can put together the essence of the thing from a maze of common and statute law. But even these experts do not really 'know their rights', since rights subtly and constantly change in response to a curious political economy of supply and demand.

A free country? Freedom is to be able to gather together in a room above the public bar to promote a revolution. It is for several thousand people preaching that revolution to be able to march through a city without being shot at, beaten up or arrested without cause. It is for passport-holding citizens to be able to come and go at will. It is for magazine editors to be able to publish foul-mouthed political nonsense without risk of fine or imprisonment.

Our rights are to know that the police cannot come crashing through the door at six in the morning just because they are suspicious of our politics. To know that we cannot be picked up and detained indefinitely, without a lawyer being allowed to see us. To know that we will not go to prison without being heard, and that the judge, jury and prosecution will never be the same people.

Our rights extend equally to all of us, whether we are male or female, black or white, Protestant or Catholic. They cannot be taken away by men in white coats with syringes, or by soldiers with rifles. We cannot lose our jobs because of our religious or political beliefs.

That catechism is a reasonable, though not exclusive, characterization of
civil liberty in Britain. Yet in the early 1970s, only the first of those dozen
tenets was absolutely true (and then only if Ulster is not considered). In 1970,
Cambridge students were arrested and gaoled merely for taking part in a
demonstration (again, to ignore the infinitely more serious matter of the
thirteen unarmed demonstrators killed by the paratroopers in Londonderry
in 1972). In 1971 and 1972, British citizens from East Africa were
shuttlecocked around the world to discourage them coming to the country
which issued them with passports. In 1971, the three editors of *Oz* were sent
to gaol. In 1972, after the Aldershot bombing, the homes of sixty people
were raided simply because they were known to hold Left-wing views. In
the same year, a police inspector admitted keeping a man in the cells for a
week without charging him. In 1970, more than nine out of ten cases heard
by the Bootle magistrates were dealt with without a defence lawyer. In
1969, there were more than 10,000 complaints against the police, all of them
investigated and judged by the police themselves: in all but 235 of them,
they decided they were innocent.

(Barry Cox, *Civil Liberties in Britain*)

encapsulated: summarized
fuzzy: unclear
maze: labyrinth, very complicated structure
subtly: in a way that is difficult to analyse
foul-mouthed: disgusting
catechism: list of questions and answers
tenets: principles
Ulster: Northern Ireland
gaoled: (= jailed) put in prison
shuttlecocked: sent backwards and forwards (a shuttlecock is a cork with feathers in,
used in badminton)

Human rights for everyone

The main Declaration of Rights, covering human rights for all people, was
proclaimed by the United Nations in 1948. *The Universal Declaration of
Human Rights, 1948*, has thirty articles. These are some of the most important.

All human beings are born free and equal in dignity and rights.
Everyone is entitled to all the rights and freedoms set forth in the
    Declaration without distinction of any kind, such as race, colour, sex,
    language, religion, political or other opinion, national or social origin,
    property, birth or other status.
Everyone has the right to life, liberty and security of person.
No one shall be held in slavery or servitude.

No one shall be subjected to torture or to cruelty, inhuman or degrading
   treatment or punishment.
Everyone has the right to recognition everywhere as a person before the law.
No one shall be subjected to arbitrary arrest, detention or exile.
Everyone charged with a penal offence has the right to be presumed
   innocent until proved guilty according to law in a public trial at which
   he has had all the guarantees necessary for his defence.
No one shall be subjected to arbitrary interference with his privacy, family,
   home or correspondence, nor attacks upon his honour and reputation.
Everyone has the right to seek and to enjoy in other countries asylum from
   persecution.

(Nan Berger, *Rights*)

dignity: human value
degrading: reducing a person's human value
arbitrary: without reason
exile: being forced to live abroad
asylum: protection

You know what I mean

COUNTRY JOE: Give me an F!
AUDIENCE: F!
COUNTRY JOE: Thank you. About two years ago I was still with The Fish and
   we played Worcester, Massachusetts, and did the 'Fuck Cheer' like we
   usually do – or did – and nothing particularly strange happened, and then
   we went to Boston, played the Boston Garden next day. What we didn't
   know was the Worcester police had called the Boston police and told
   them we were coming. And when we got there we were met by
   seventy-five uniformed police officers with guns, clubs and mace, three
   lieutenants, one captain, twenty-five plain-clothes men and a guy in a
   trench-coat, three squad cars and a paddy-wagon. And they wanted to
   know where I was, and they finally found me, and the captain said to me
   that he wanted me to know that this wasn't Worcester, you know. I told
   him I knew that, I knew it was Boston. He said 'Well, uh, we just wanted
   to tell you not to say it here.' I said 'What's it?' He said 'You know what
   I mean.' I said 'No, I – I don't know what you mean.' He said 'Yeah, you
   know what I mean.' I said 'No, I don't know what you mean.' He said
   'Yeah, you know what I mean.' I said 'No, I don't know what you
   mean.'
   So the lieutenant took me aside and explained to me what was
happening, you know, he said 'Don't say it here.' I said 'What's it?'

He said 'You know what I mean.' I said 'No, I don't know what you mean.' He said 'Yeah, you know what I mean.'

We did that for a long time, you know. And I knew what they meant, you know, but I wanted to hear them say it, but I didn't know, it was my own ignorance, 'cause I didn't know at that particular time that they have a – a law in Massachusetts that cops can't say 'fuck' on duty. Uh, so finally the captain just said that if we did anything that they didn't like they'd beat us up and take us to jail. So I said 'I know what you mean.'

We got on stage, and there was thirty cops over here, and thirty cops over there, and the captain marching back and forth, back and forth, watching us, you know. Behind us twenty-five plain-clothes men and a guy in a trench-coat – I – I don't know if they were plain-clothes men or not you know, but it's the only concert I've ever played where there was twenty-five guys who all looked alike standing behind me, you know.

And we didn't say 'fuck' that night because we weren't feeling, uh, masochistic, you know. And so, after it was all over with, they – they thanked us a lot and said we could come back any time we wanted to. And we said 'Fuck you'.

Country Joe McDonald

The Fish: a group of musicians
mace: a gas used by American police for riot control
squad cars: police cars
paddy-wagon: (slang) car for transporting prisoners who are under arrest
cops: (slang) policemen

Taboo words

Generally, the type of word that is tabooed in a particular language will be a good reflection of at least part of the system of values and beliefs of the society in question. In some communities, word-magic plays an important part in religion, and certain words regarded as powerful will be used in spells and incantations. In different parts of the world taboo words include those for the left hand, for female relations, or for certain game animals. Some words, too, are much more severely tabooed than others. In the English-speaking world, the most severe taboos are now associated with words connected with sex, closely followed by those connected with excretion and the Christian religion. This is a reflection of the great emphasis traditionally placed on sexual morality in our culture. In other, particularly Roman Catholic, cultures the strongest taboos may be associated with religion, and in Norway, for example, some of the most strongly tabooed expressions are concerned with the devil.

Until recently, the strict rules associated with some taboo words in English received legal as well as social reinforcement. Not so long ago, the use in print of words such as *fuck* and *cunt* could lead to prosecution and even imprisonment, and they are still not widely used in newspapers. Laws of this type have been relaxed in Britain and America, but there are still some parts of the English-speaking world where this is not the case. It may be unwise even now to use such words in public in Britain, although at least one magistrate has ruled that '*fuck*' is no longer obscene, i.e. legally tabooed.

There is, of course, a certain amount of 'double-think' about words of this type. Although their use was, and may still be, technically illegal in some cases, they occur very frequently in the speech of some sections of the community. This is largely because taboo-words are frequently used as swear-words, which is in turn because they are *powerful*. Most people in modern technologically advanced societies would claim not to believe in magic. There is still, however, something that very closely resembles magic surrounding the use of taboo-words in English. The use of taboo-words in non-permitted contexts, such as on television, provokes violent reaction, of apparently very real shock and disgust. The reaction, moreover, is an irrational reaction to a particular word, not to a concept. It is perfectly permissible to say 'sexual intercourse' on television. Taboo is therefore clearly a linguistic as well as sociological fact. It is the words themselves which are felt to be wrong and are therefore so powerful.

(Peter Trudgill, *Sociolinguistics*)

taboo: primitive custom or religious law which forbids the use of certain words, performance of certain actions, etc.
spells and incantations: magic formulas
game animals: animals hunted for food
swear-words: 'bad' words used to express anger or other strong emotions
concept: idea
in order: acceptable

157

"Why can't you just swear like any other man?"

'The first time I got arrested for obscenity was in San Francisco. I used a ten-letter word on stage. Just a word in passing. 'Lenny, I want to talk to you', the police officer said. 'You're under arrest. That word you said – you can't say that in a public place. It's against the law.'

(Lenny Bruce in *Getting Busted*)

obscenity: words or actions regarded as disgusting (particularly in relation to sex)
ten-letter word: Lenny Bruce used the word 'cocksucker' (a slang word for *homosexual*)

Violence in the cinema

The Texas Chainsaw Massacre, too, touches on cannibalism, and is also allegedly based on a true story, the story of a demented Texas family that slaughtered practically every passer-by within reach and cut up the bodies and sold them in pies. At present it has only a GLC X certificate, which means it can't be seen outside London, and this of course is because of its excessive violence. It seems to me that the increasing emphasis on violence on the screen ought to be a matter for concern. The sight of someone being hacked to death is surely far more obscene, and indeed pornographic, than the sight of two people making gentle love to each other, although for reasons that I find unfathomable it is only the love scenes that whip the self-appointed moralists among us into a state of hysterical outrage. Anyway, the point I wish to make is that an almost drooling relish in the physical details of violent death is the most objectionable feature of a new British picture called *Schizo* – an abbreviation of schizophrenia, which, as a disembodied voice on the film very kindly points out, is a disease of the mind. *Schizo*, I think, is meant to be a thriller after Hitchcock, although it's so far after Hitchcock that even on *Concorde* it could never catch up. Lynn Frederick plays a newly married ice-skater, apparently pursued with murderous intent by an ex-convict who'd served time for killing her mother, and in the course of the action, three vicious murders are shown in lingering and quite unnecessary detail. That apart, it's the kind of film that depends heavily on the total obtuseness of all concerned. If there'd been anyone around with a high enough IQ to be able to tie his own bootlaces without too much outside help, the entire mystery could have been cleared up in five minutes.

(*Film 76* on BBC1 TV)

cannibalism: eating human flesh
demented: mad
slaughtered: killed
GLC: Greater London Council
X certificate: permission for a film to be shown to adult audiences
hacked: cut
unfathomable: impossible to understand
whip: arouse

outrage: moralistic anger
drooling: with the mouth watering
relish: enjoyment
after Hitchcock: in imitation of Hitchcock
served time: been in prison
lingering: slow-moving
obtuseness: stupidity
IQ: intelligence quotient (a measure of intelligence)

Censorship

WHY does Mary Whitehouse think that dirty films are going to corrupt me, when she seems able to see them—or at least read the scripts — without their having any effect on her?

I do not entirely

(*Daily Mirror*)

disagree with her campaign and I don't like the current vogue of sex with everything, but I exercise my own censorship.

I simply don't go to see the film.—P. Gordon, London NW2.

campaign: movement (to clean up television)
vogue: fashion

159

*"Having read this truly appalling book,
I give as my considered opinion that it
is definitely calculated to deprave
and corrupt."*

The meal that cost ten weeks

Last August 5, Jim Young and Kevin Bates, two north Londoners in their early twenties, sat down to a dinner of steak, peas and chips in the Angus Steak House, Charing Cross Road. They had a few whiskies with the meal, lingered over the dessert and paid the £12 bill with a Barclaycard.

Last week, nearly three months later, they were released from Pentonville Prison. Both had been remanded in custody, charged with 'obtaining a meal by deceit', after police had opposed bail at their hearing at Bow Street magristrates court. And last Tuesday, on the day of their release, they were put on probation after being found guilty at Knightsbridge Crown Court. But, in effect, they both served a ten-week sentence *before* they had actually been tried for the offence.

In addition, Kevin Bates claims

that he was twice beaten up. And both men are so angry at the way in which they and the 89 other unconvicted prisoners were treated that they are petitioning MP Ron Brown of Hackney to press for a full investigation.

The Young-Bates case is just the tip of the massive 'unconvicted prisoners' iceberg. There are at the moment 3,442 unconvicted male prisoners and 131 unconvicted female prisoners in jails up and down the country. Last year alone, 49,776 men and 3,191 women were held in prison to await their trial. Some were in for only a few days, but a number spent up to nine or ten months and the average stay is 25 days. And the figures are increasing: a survey by Camberwell Magistrates Court showed that during the decade 1964-74 the number of convicted people in prison rose by 17%, but the number of unconvicted people in prison rose by *157%*!

Nor are the prisoners held necessarily charged with violent or serious crimes; the majority are awaiting trial on small theft charges or minor offences. Most are unable to raise the bail or are not represented in court when the police oppose the granting of bail. Almost half of them are eventually found not guilty or are given non-custodial sentences.

'We came up in court last week,' says Young. 'By that time we had spent ten weeks in nick, lost our flat in Edmonton, had our clothes stolen from it because there was no one there and had our car towed off because the tax ran out in August. And that was all before we even went up for trial . . .'
(Duncan Campbell)

(Kevin Tilfourd, *Time Out* 5 – 11 November 1976)

Barclaycard: banker's card that guarantees payment of a cheque
remanded in custody: sent to prison to wait for trial
deceit: telling lies
opposed bail: asked for them not to be released until the trial
put on probation: released on condition that they did not commit further crimes
tip of the iceberg: small visible part of a very large problem
raise the bail: find the money necessary as a guarantee for someone released on bail
non-custodial sentences: punishment that does not involve prison
nick: (slang) prison
towed off: pulled away (by the police)

"Stayed in all day . . ."

Teedom

It's a great thing to go to jail for right, but whether you're there for right or wrong, when you hear that big steel door close and that key turn, you know you're there. That was Birmingham, May of 1963. Martin Luther King asked me to come down. I arrived at 11:30 a.m. on a Monday, and an hour and a half later I went to jail with more than 800 other demonstrators. It was my first time in jail to stay.

'You Dick Gregory?'

'I'm Mister Gregory.'

Somebody snatched my collar and my feet didn't hit the floor again until I was in solitary confinement.

Later in the afternoon I was brought downstairs and put in a cell built for twenty-five people. There must have been 500 of us in there. When they moved us out to eat, the corridors were so crowded you couldn't walk. Just stand still and let the crowd move you along. The last one back in the cell didn't have a place to lie down and sleep.

There was a little boy, maybe four years old, standing in the corner of the cell sucking his thumb. I felt sorry for him. He didn't even have someone his age to play with. I kind of rubbed his head and asked him how he was.

'All right,' he said.

'What are you here for?'

'Teedom,' he said. Couldn't even say Freedom but he was in jail for it.

(Dick Gregory, 'Nigger' in *Getting Busted*)

Birmingham: Birmingham, Alabama, scene of civil rights demonstrations
Martin Luther King: black civil rights leader, later assassinated
in solitary confinement: locked up alone

Take this hammer

Take this hammer, carry it to the captain
Take this hammer, carry it to the captain
Take this hammer, carry it to the captain
Tell him I'm gone, tell him I'm gone.

If he asks you was I running (*three times*)
Tell him I was flying, tell him I was flying.

If he asks you was I laughing (*three times*)
Tell him I was crying, tell him I was crying.

I don't want no cornbread or tomatoes (*three times*)
They hurts my pride, they hurts my pride.

I'm gonna bust right, bust right past that shooter (*three times*)
I'm going home, I'm going home.

(Prison work song)

bust: (slang) break out violently   *shooter:* (slang) guard

A prisoner's timetable

I was locked behind the door most of the time for 16 hours of the day. My time was – that I used to get up at 7 o'clock in the morning; slop out, that's empty your water-pot and your wash-bowl and all that sort of thing; you're banged up again; they open you up at about half seven, you go down for your breakfast, and then you come up and they lock you up again. And in that time from breakfast to eight o'clock you eat your breakfast, wash and shave. And then they come round at eight o'clock, open you up again, collect the razor-blades – because you don't keep your own razor-blades, they issue them daily, and then they take them back. And then at eight o'clock – well, I used to be early work, most of the fellows never started work until half past nine – quarter past eight I used to go to work, and work in the dry cleaner's till half past ten, with nineteen other fellows. And then we went out on an hour's exercise, till half past eleven, but you never used to get exercise if it was raining.

And then at half past eleven you go back to your wing, you get your dinner and then you go back to your cell. You eat your meals in your cell, they don't have dining out in Wandsworth. And at half past eleven you're banged up till one o'clock. And at one o'clock you put your meal tray out, so they come round and collect it, and then you slop out again – that's empty

163

your pot if you happen to use the toilet – and then they bang you up again till half past one, and then you go back to work at half past one – that's what used to happen to me, anyway – and then you work right the way through to half past four. Then you come in at half past four, you get your water and all that ready for the night, and make your bed and that, and then at five o'clock you go down for your tea. And then from five o'clock until the morning at seven o'clock I used to be banged up, locked up behind the door.

You get a film once a fortnight and a concert once a fortnight. And that's usually on a weekend. Otherwise if you've got no concert or a film you're locked up all weekend except for your hour's exercise. We have visitors once a month – in Wandsworth you have visitors once a month, but after you've done a year of your sentence, you're allowed two visitors a month – but they're only a half-hour visit.

(Extract from an interview with Michael, an ex-prisoner)

banged up: (slang) locked up
dry cleaner's: place where clothes are cleaned

Executioner

[Britain had capital punishment (the death penalty) for murder and some other crimes until 1965. This is an extract from the autobiography of Albert Pierrepoint, who was official executioner from 1931 to 1956.]

I looked round the green-painted execution chamber to check that everything was in order. I picked up a stray thread of twine from where it had fallen on the traps. With a piece of chalk I re-lined the T-mark under the noose on the front drop where the prisoner's toes were to be aligned, the arches of the feet directly over the crack in the doors. I slightly shifted the cross-planks on either side of the T, and I made one final adjustment. I crossed to the lever and released a split pin that held the cotter pin fast, and I eased out the cotter pin for half its length, so that, while still resisting an untimely push, the end of it was flush with the side of the lever. In action, even the time it took to withdraw an extra half-inch was important to me.

'Right,' I said. 'Breakfast.' And we went away for bacon and eggs.

At five minutes to nine we were given the signal that the Sheriff had gone to the Governor's office. Wade and I walked across the prison yard with an officer who led us up to the corridor outside the condemned cell. I think the next minutes of waiting were the worst, not only then but on every occasion. It is impossible not to feel apprehension and even fear at the prospect of the responsibility of the moment, but with me the frailty passed as soon as there was action. At half a minute to nine a small group came down the corridor. There was the Sheriff, the Governor, the doctor and some senior prison officers. I suddenly had a strange realisation. I was the youngest man there, and the eyes of everyone were on me. The party paused at the next door to that of the condemned cell, the door of the execution chamber. A finger was raised and they passed in. The chief opened the door of the cell and I went forward with a strap in my hand.

The prisoner was standing, facing me, smiling. In his civilian clothes he looked as smart as I had already registered him. In my civilian clothes, amid all those uniforms, we might have been meeting for a chat in a club in Leicester Square – but who would have foreseen a robed priest in the room? I quickly strapped his wrists and said 'Follow me.'

The door in the side wall of the cell had been opened as I came in, and I walked through it into the execution chamber. He followed me, walking seven paces with the noose straight ahead of him, and the escorting officers mounting the crossplanks gently stopped him as he stood on the T. I had turned in time to face him. Eye to eye, that last look. Wade was stooping behind him, swiftly fastening the ankle strap. I pulled from my breast pocket the white cap, folded as carefully as a parachute, and drew it down over his head. 'Cheerio', he said. I reached for the noose, pulled it down over the cap, tightened it to my right, pulled a rubber washer along the rope to hold it, and darted to my left, crouching towards the cotter pin at the base of the lever. I was in the position of a sprinter at the start of a race as I went over the cross-plank, pulled the pin with one hand, and pushed the lever with the other, instinctively looking back as I did so. There was a snap as the falling doors were bitten and held by the rubber clips, and the rope stood straight and still. The broken twine spooned down in a falling leaf, passed through a little eddy of dust, and floated into the pit.

I went to the side of the scaffold and walked down into the pit. I undid the prisoner's shirt for the stethoscope, and the doctor followed me. I came up again, and waited. The doctor came back to the scaffold. 'Everything is all right,' he said. It was a curious way for a doctor to pronounce death. I suppose his intention was to reassure the Governor, and possibly me.

We all left the execution chamber. Soon the Governor sent for me. 'I have seen your uncle work on many occasions,' he said. 'He is a very good man indeed. Never has he been any quicker than you have been this morning.'

(*Executioner: Pierrepoint*)

twine: thin string
traps: trapdoors (doors in the floor)
noose: loop of rope which is put round the victim's neck
cotter pin: pin that stops the lever moving
flush: level

frailty: weakness
darted: moved quickly
eddy: circular movement
stethoscope: doctor's instrument for listening to the heartbeat

A hanging

[The famous writer George Orwell (author of *1984* and *Animal Farm*) worked for several years in the Colonial Police in Burma. This is an extract from a piece in which he describes how he was forced to witness an execution.]

It was about forty yards to the gallows. I watched the bare brown back of the prisoner marching in front of me. He walked clumsily with his bound arms, but quite steadily, with that bobbing gait of the Indian who never straightens his knees. At each step his muscles slid neatly into place, the lock of hair on his scalp danced up and down, his feet printed themselves on the wet gravel. And once, in spite of the men who gripped him by each shoulder, he stepped slightly aside to avoid a puddle on the path.

It is curious, but till that moment I had never realized what it means to destroy a healthy, conscious man. When I saw the prisoner step aside to avoid the puddle, I saw the mystery, the unspeakable wrongness, of cutting a life short when it is in full tide. This man was not dying, he was alive just as we were alive. All the organs of his body were working – bowels digesting food, skin renewing itself, nails growing, tissues forming – all toiling away in solemn foolery. His nails would still be growing when he stood on the drop, when he was falling through the air with a tenth of a second to live. His eyes saw the yellow gravel and the grey walls, and his brain still remembered, foresaw, reasoned – reasoned even about puddles. He and we were a party of men walking together, seeing, hearing, feeling, understanding the same world; and in two minutes, with a sudden snap, one of us would be gone – one mind less, one world less.

George Orwell

gallows: construction for hanging condemned men
bound: tied
bobbing: moving up and down
gait: way of walking
puddle: small pool of water
toiling: working hard

When I came back to Dublin, I was courtmartialled in my absence and sentenced to death in my absence, so I said they could shoot me in my absence.

Brendan Behan

courtmartialled: tried by a military court

Heads, heads, heads, heads, heads

[Rosencrantz and Guildenstern are two minor characters in Shakespeare's Hamlet – they attempt to betray Hamlet, he finds out and causes them to be executed. Tom Stoppard has given them a play of their own; it begins with their slow realization, as they toss a coin which always comes down heads, that they cannot any longer be in the natural world.]

ACT ONE

Two ELIZABETHANS *passing the time in a place without any visible character.*

> *They are well dressed – hats, cloaks, sticks and all.*
> *Each of them has a large leather money bag.*
> GUILDENSTERN'*s bag is nearly empty.*
> ROSENCRANTZ'*s bag is nearly full.*
> *The reason being: they are betting on the toss of a coin, in the following manner:* GUILDENSTERN (*hereafter* 'GUIL') *takes a coin out of his bag, spins it, letting it fall.* ROSENCRANTZ (*hereafter* 'ROS') *studies it, announces it as* 'heads' (*as it happens*) *and puts it into his own bag. Then they repeat the process. They have apparently been doing this for some time.*
> *The run of* 'heads' *is impossible, yet* ROS *betrays no surprise at all – he feels none. However, he is nice enough to feel a little embarrassed at taking so much money off his friend. Let that be his character note.*
> GUIL *is well alive to the oddity of it. He is not worried about the money, but he is worried by the implications; aware but not going to panic about it – his character note.*
> GUIL *sits.* ROS *stands* (*he does the moving, retrieving coins*).
> GUIL *spins.* ROS *studies coin.*

ROS: Heads.
> (*He picks it up and puts it in his bag. The process is repeated.*)
> Heads.
> (*Again.*)
ROS: Heads.
> (*Again.*)
> Heads.
> (*Again.*)
> Heads.
GUIL (*flipping a coin*): There is an art to the building up of suspense.
ROS: Heads.
GUIL: (*flipping another*): Though it can be done by luck alone.
ROS: Heads.
GUIL: If that's the word I'm after.

ROS: (*raises his head at* GUIL): Seventy-six love.

> (GUIL *gets up but has nowhere to go. He spins another coin over his shoulder without looking at it, his attention being directed at his environment or lack of it.* Heads.

GUIL: A weaker man might be moved to re-examine his faith, if in nothing else at least in the law of probability.

> (*He slips a coin over his shoulder as he goes to look upstage.*)

ROS: Heads

   . . .

GUIL: Are you happy?

ROS: What?

GUIL: Content? At ease?

ROS: I suppose so.

GUIL: What are you going to do now?

ROS: I don't know. What do you want to do?

GUIL: I have no desires. None. (*He stops pacing dead.*) There was a messenger . . . that's right. We were sent for. (*He wheels at* ROS *and raps out* –) . . . One, probability is a factor which operates within natural forces. Two, probability is not operating as a factor. Three, we are now within un-, sub- or supernatural forces. Discuss. (ROS *is suitably startled* – *Acidly.*) Not too heatedly.

(Tom Stoppard, *Rosencrantz and Guildenstern are dead*)

Elizabethans: people living at the time of Queen Elizabeth I (1558–1603)
oddity: strangeness
the implications: what it means
aware: conscious of what is going on
retrieving: getting back
seventy-six love: seventy-six to Rosencrantz, zero to Guildenstern
environment: surroundings
upstage: away from the audience
stops dead: stops suddenly
wheels: turns quickly
raps out: says very quickly

Probability

Heads and tails in coin-tossing offer an instance of equal probabilities. (So do certain wagers on a roulette wheel – the bets on red or black or even or odd or the first or the second half of the numbers. The roulette case is complicated, however, by the fact that the odds are not *quite* even, so let's stick to coin-tossing for a while and go into roulette later.)

To find the probability of any sequence of occurrence in coin-tossing or other equal-odds situation, you need only list all the possibilities and then count up the ones that meet your requirement.

Making the list is simple enough if you tackle it systematically. Using H and T to stand for heads and tails, the two possible results of one toss become H and T. For two tosses, add successively an H and a T to each of the first two. This will give you HH, TH, HT, TT. For a sequence of three tosses, add successively H and T to each of those four. And so on.

The picture shows how you can easily do this by making one column after another of alternating Hs and Ts, doubling the number each time. Connect as shown, and read by starting with the first column and following the connecting links across until you have used each letter in the last column to end a sequence.

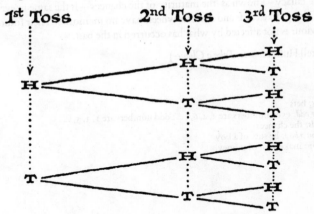

For some calculations, such as the likelihood of children (or heads and tails in coin-tossing) coming out fifty-fifty or in some other specific ratio, there is no really simple alternative to listing in this manner . . .

For other things you can apply rules . . . One rule: To find the probability of getting all of several different things, multiply together the chances of getting each one.

What, for instance, is the likelihood of tossing heads any given number of times in a row? For one toss we've noted that the chance is one half. For two tosses it is one half times one half, or one fourth. For ten tosses it is the product of one half taken ten times, which is about .00098, or a little less than one chance in a thousand.

From this it follows that if you want all of quite a few things and each of them is only fairly likely, your chance of getting them all is slight.

The number of cases, or size of sample, is fundamental to all sorts of applications of probability theory, and we shall come back to it frequently.

This brings us to the influence of history on chances, the most likely source of errors and confusion of all. The argument takes many forms:

'I've been holding terrible cards all evening. By the law of averages I should get very good hands from now on.'

'It has rained nearly every day during the first half of May. Since on the average only half the days in May are wet in this climate, we can expect dry weather the rest of the month.'

'We've had four girls in a row. Since the chances are 31 to one against five successive girls, we can practically count on a boy if we try again.'

'I've kept a record on this roulette wheel for a month, and it has come up red 123 times more than black. Since by the law of averages red and black show up equally often, I can now clean up by betting on the black.'

The fallacy – known as 'the maturity of the chances' – is the same in every case. Things like cards and roulette wheels have no memories. Their future behaviour is not affected by what has occurred in the past.

(Darrell Huff, *How to Take a Chance*)

wagers: bets
even or odd: even numbers are 2, 4, 6, . . .; odd numbers are 1, 3, 5, . . .
the odds: the chances
count on a boy: be sure of a boy
clean up: make a lot of money

Mathematical quickies

[Answers are on page 173.]

From head to foot

A number of pigs, a number of geese, a farmer and his one-legged son were in a field. Altogether there were 17 heads and 39 feet. How many geese were there?

Early and late

'The last time I did this trip,' said the engine-driver, 'I averaged 45 mph, and arrived at my destination five minutes too soon. This time I averaged 40 mph, and arrived five minutes late.'

What was the distance of the trip?

Nine all

Can you find the smallest number which, if you multiply it by seven, will give an answer consisting entirely of nines?

Amy's age

Multiply together a half, a third and a quarter of Amy's age, and the product will be 576.

How old *is* Amy?

Queer currency

In the country of Pulmania, the planka is worth fourpence. The plinka, on the other hand, is worth as much as a planka plus a plonka. A planka and a plinka are equal to five plonkas, and a plinka and a plonka make a plunka.

How much is each unit worth?

product: result of a multiplication

Mathematics: algebra and its language

If a car travels for two hours at 60 miles per hour it covers 120 miles. Similarly, a car moving at 50 miles per hour for three hours travels 150 miles. The distance is obtained by multiplying the velocity by the time.

This statement can be written in a much shorter way if symbols are used instead of words. If distance is represented by the letter s, velocity by the letter v, and time by t, then we can write $s = v \times t$. We usually do not bother to include the multiplication sign and simply write $s = vt$. This type of expression belongs to algebra, a branch of mathematics which was invented by the Arabs. The word comes from the Arabic 'Al jebr' meaning the great art.

Algebra is a form of language for writing about numbers and measurements and the relationships between them. Not only is it much shorter than using words but it helps in working out mathematical problems. For example, in the equation $s = vt$, everything on the left of the equals sign is equal to everything on the right. We can do anything to one side as long as we do the same to the other. For example,

if both sides are divided by v we get $\dfrac{s}{v} = \dfrac{vt}{v}$ or $t = \dfrac{s}{v}$; i.e. the time

taken is the distance divided by the velocity.

A more complicated example would be a problem such as 'in two years' time a man will be twice as old as his son is now. If their total age is 67, how old is the son?'

First we translate the words into symbols. If m stands for the man's age in years, then in two years' time he will be m + 2 years old. Now we can construct our first equation: $m + 2 = 2s$, where s is the son's age. We now have one equation, but two unknown symbols, i.e. m and s. In order to solve the equation, that is to assign values to the symbols, we must always have the same number of equations as we have unknowns. In this case, therefore, we need one more equation: it is $m + s = 67$. If $m + 2 = 2s$ we can subtract 2 from each side and get $m = 2s - 2$. We can now use this value of m in the equation $m + s = 67$. Adding up the $2s + s$ on the left-hand side and putting the numbers on the right we get $3s = 69$, or $s = 23$. The son's age, therefore, is 23.

(*Penguin Book of the Physical World*)

velocity: speed
symbols: signs
assign: give

Mathematical quickies

[Answers to mathematical problems on page 171.]

From head to foot: 12
Early and late: 60 miles
nine all: 142,857
Amy's age: 24
Queer currency: A plinka = 6p, a plonka = 2p, a plunka = 8p

How to prove that 2 = 1

1. Suppose that $a = b$.
   Multiply by a. Then:
2. $a^2 = ab$.
   Subtract b^2. Then:
3. $a^2 - b^2 = ab - b^2$.
   But $a^2 - b^2$ is the same as $(a + b)(a - b)$.
   And $ab - b^2$ is the same as $b(a - b)$.
   So:
4. $(a + b)(a - b) = b(a - b)$.
   Divide by $(a - b)$. Then:
5. $a + b = b$.
   But $a = b$; therefore $a + b = 2b$. So:
6. $2b = b$.
   Divide by b. Then:
7. $2 = 1$.

Test your IQ

[This is part of an 'IQ' test – a test designed to show a person's 'intelligence quotient'. Tests of this kind were at one time an important part of the '11 +' exam, which determined whether a child would go to a grammar school or not. They were also sometimes used for job selection. The use of IQ tests has been criticized a good deal, and they are less frequently used nowadays. The answers to the questions are on page 176.]

1. Insert the missing number.

    25   20   15   10   __

2. Underline the odd-man-out.

chariot car bus waggon sleigh

3. Insert the missing number.

3 7 16 35 __

4. Underline the odd-man-out.

ant spider bee moth midge

5. Underline which of these animals whose names are hidden in the jumbled letters below is the smallest.

NOBIS
NETIKT
WROTHAG
USEOM
IRGAFFE

6. Insert a word which means the same as the two words outside the brackets.

disc (. . . . . .) achievement

7. Which of the six numbered figures on the opposite page fits into the vacant space? (Insert the number in the square.)

8. Insert the word that completes the first word and starts the second.

SP (. . .) EAR

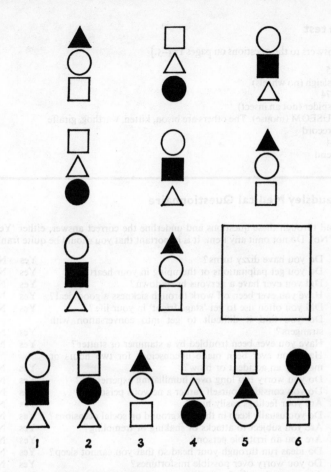

1   2   3   4   5   6

(H. J. Eysenck, *Know Your Own IQ*)

IQ test

[Answers to the questions on pages 173–5.]

1. 5
2. sleigh (no wheels)
3. 74
4. spider (not an insect)
5. USEOM (mouse). The others are bison, kitten, warthog, giraffe
6. record
7. 4
8. end

Maudsley Medical Questionnaire

Read through these questions and underline the correct answer, either 'Yes' or 'No'. Do not omit any item. It is important that you should be quite frank.

1.	Do you have dizzy turns?	Yes	No
2.	Do you get palpitations or thumping in your heart?	Yes	No
3.	Did you ever have a nervous breakdown?	Yes	No
4.	Have you ever been off work through sickness a good deal?	Yes	No
5.	Did you often use to get 'stage fright' in your life?	Yes	No
6.	Do you find it difficult to get into conversation with strangers?	Yes	No
7.	Have you ever been troubled by a stammer or stutter?	Yes	No
8.	Have you ever been made unconscious for two hours or more by an accident or blow?	Yes	No
9.	Do you worry too long over humiliating experiences?	Yes	No
10.	Do you consider yourself rather a nervous person?	Yes	No
11.	Are your feelings easily hurt?	Yes	No
12.	Do you usually keep in the background on social occasions?	Yes	No
13.	Are you subject to attacks of shaking or trembling?	Yes	No
14.	Are you an irritable person?	Yes	No
15.	Do ideas run through your head so that you cannot sleep?	Yes	No
16.	Do you worry over possible misfortunes?	Yes	No
17.	Are you rather shy?	Yes	No
18.	Do you sometimes feel happy, sometimes depressed, without any apparent reason?	Yes	No
19.	Do you daydream a lot?	Yes	No
20.	Do you seem to have less life about you than others?	Yes	No
21.	Do you sometimes get a pain over your heart?	Yes	No
22.	Do you have nightmares?	Yes	No
23.	Do you worry about your health?	Yes	No
24.	Have you sometimes walked in your sleep?	Yes	No
25.	Do you sweat a great deal without exercise?	Yes	No
26.	Do you find it difficult to make friends?	Yes	No
27.	Does your mind often wander badly, so that you lose track of what you are doing?	Yes	No
28.	Are you touchy on various subjects?	Yes	No
29.	Do you often feel disgruntled?	Yes	No

30.	Do you often feel just miserable?	Yes	No
31.	Do you often feel self-conscious in the presence of your superiors?	Yes	No
32.	Do you suffer from sleeplessness?	Yes	No
33.	Did you ever get short of breath without having done heavy work?	Yes	No
34.	Do you ever suffer from severe headaches?	Yes	No
35.	Do you suffer from 'nerves'?	Yes	No
36.	Are you troubled by aches and pains?	Yes	No
37.	Do you get nervous in places such as lifts, trains, or tunnels?	Yes	No
38.	Do you suffer from attacks of diarrhoea?	Yes	No
39.	Do you lack self-confidence?	Yes	No
40.	Are you troubled with feelings of inferiority?	Yes	No

The score is simply the number of 'Yes's' underlined by the subject. The average score of groups of normal subjects is about 10, that of neurotics about 20. (The reader should not take it too much to heart if, on going through the questionnaire, he finds that he gives 20 or more 'Yes' answers. This does not mean that he is a neurotic. Inventories of this kind can give useful leads to the experienced psychologist and they may single out people for further investigation; in themselves they should never in any circumstances be used to arrive at a conclusion about a person's mental health.)

(H. J. Eysenck, *Sense and Nonsense in Psychology*)

dizzy turn: feeling that everything is going round, or that you are about to faint
palpitations: very rapid heart-beats
stammer, stutter: speech defect; repeating the same sound against one's will ('C-c-c-come here')
humiliating experiences: events that make you feel ridiculous
lose track of: forget
touchy: irritable, easily angered
disgruntled: bad-tempered because of unfair treatment
diarrhoea: digestive problem which makes you go to the lavatory very often
inventories: lists

(*Psychology Today*)

psychosomatic disorders: physical troubles which have a psychological origin
phobias: irrational fears (for instance, of spiders)
compulsions: irrational need to do certain actions (for instance, washing one's hands very often)
migraines: kind of very severe headache

June and her parents

[The well-known psychiatrist R. D. Laing believes that many cases of mental disturbance are the result of destructive family relationships. Here is an extract from his study of one case.]

In the period of recovery, almost every advance made by June (in the viewpoint of nursing staff, psychiatric social worker, occupational therapists, and ourselves) was opposed vehemently by her mother, who consistently regarded as steps back what to us and to June were steps forward.

Here are a few examples.

June began to take some initiative. Her mother expressed great alarm at any such show either on the grounds that June was irresponsible, or that it was not like June to do anything without asking. It was not that there was anything wrong in what June did, it was that she did not ask permission first.

INTERVIEWER: What do you perceive as being wrong with June this weekend?

MOTHER: Well on Saturday for instance, June wanted to go to the Youth Club – well she went down to the Youth Club and that was all right, I didn't mind her going. Well I went in to attend to Grandad, and then I saw June coming down the road with two boys from up the road, she had no coat on – June has a shocking cold in her head this weekend and you know how cold it was on Saturday – and so I went and called after her of course and asked her where she was going and she was going with Eric to the – to a dance at the Church Hall. Well I knew *nothing* about it at all.

JUNE: (voice raised) Well *I* didn't until I went and called round.

MOTHER: Yes I know, but I would expect you June to *come and say* where you were going.

JUNE: Well I'd have been back at the same time as I'd come back from the ordinary Youth Club, so I didn't see any reason for –

MOTHER: You wouldn't have come back at all.

JUNE: (indignant) I *would* have done!

MOTHER: June you would *not*. You couldn't possibly come back from the dance in the time that you usually come back.

JUNE: Well I don't know. I was home at nine o'clock from the other place.

MOTHER: And in any case you had no money to go to the dance or anything –

JUNE: Well Eric would have lent me some, it would have been all right.

FATHER: There you are you see –

MOTHER: There you are you see, how do you know that Eric even wanted to take you there?

JUNE: Well –

178

MOTHER: You went to his house, June went to his house – hunt him out –

JUNE: Well he was going to come any rate because he always comes on Saturdays.

MOTHER: Yes but he didn't go to the Youth Club, he went up to the Church Hall.

JUNE: (angrily) Yes I *know* – you don't have to tell me that a thousand times.

MOTHER: That's where I feel – you see I wouldn't have known where June was.

JUNE: Well I'd have come home at the same time as I would have come home from the Youth Club so I didn't see the need to tell her.

MOTHER: And in any case June – when you feel tired you know yourself, you just drop off to sleep – don't you?

JUNE: Mmm.

MOTHER: You just go. Well I couldn't have you going, falling asleep –

JUNE (simultaneously, inaudible) . . . well I wouldn't go falling asleep at the dance would I? What are you talking about?

MOTHER: Well I don't know what you'd have done, I only know that you fall asleep at home, you just go dead asleep – look at last weekend – you slept all Friday afternoon, all Saturday afternoon and all night, Sunday afternoon, and on Monday you were perfectly all right. You see *I* don't know whether you're going to drop off to sleep.

JUNE: Well I wouldn't have done at the dance I felt perfectly all right –

FATHER: Yes but –

MOTHER: And in any case on Saturday you *wanted* to go to bed didn't you and I said, 'Oh let's go for a walk first and then you can go to bed.' and then you decided to go to the Youth Club. Well that's perfectly all right, I don't mind June going providing I *know* where she is.

(Laing and Esterson, *Sanity, Madness and the Family*)

occupational therapist: person who helps hospital patients to find interesting activities
vehemently: violently
take some initiative: do things for herself
simultaneously: at the same time
inaudible: too quiet to be heard

Family rows

[Extract from a discussion between five schoolgirls. The letters A, C, D and E stand for the names of the girls who are speaking in this part of the discussion; words in brackets are interruptions.]

E: I think what you mainly remember is when . . . sort of . . . to your knowledge . . . your . . . the first time you see your mother and father having a row . . . Not a fight, but a row. (Yes) You always think . . . you always look at them to be . . . you know . . . you think, That's my mother and father . . . they're always so happy, you know, and I'm happy with them . . . but when you see them angry with each other . . . that just spoils everything. Sort of . . . you can't say, you know . . . then when you get older, you think, what if they got divorced . . . or had to separate . . . (Yes. Oh dear)

D: It's on your memory all the while, isn't it?

E: You think which one would you choose, and you can't . . . well, I can't . . . I couldn't choose between my mother and father.

A: They seem to be one . . . they are one. (Yeah, They are) Parents, you don't think of them as two separate people.

D: You don't split them up into mother and father . . .

A: It's when they have rows that you realize they're two separate people . . . what could go wrong. (Yes)

D: I don't want to take sides . . . I hate taking sides . . . because my mum will explain . . . she gets quite angry and she'll explain to me and tell me what happened . . . and then my dad will explain. Both the stories may be different . . . you know, the same sort of thing, but different . . . but I can see one of them isn't quite right and I can't say which one of them it is. (No)

C: Have you ever had them say . . . whichever one it is . . . say you're always on his side? (Yes)

E: I could never take sides, you know . . . if my father is . . . you know . . . shouting at my mother, I'd say, Don't shout at my mum like that! . . . and then my mother will start shouting at my dad and I'd say, Don't shout at my dad like that! . . . You know, I could never choose.

D: I can't.

A: I can remember the first row we ever had. It was . . . I think . . . my brother and I were in the kitchen and my mum and dad were rowing and it was so bad . . . I'd never seen a row like this before, and my mum just started crying her eyes out and my dad felt terribly guilty, he was dead silent. Then I started crying, my brother started crying . . . it was hell for about half an hour, you know. We all split up, there was nothing of the family left. And then we all crept back in, giggling and saying, Oh, I am sorry, you know.

D: Yes, that's the best part . . .

(James Britton, 'Talking to learn' in *Language, the Learner and the School*)

row: quarrel, angry disagreement

Patience

Dortmunder had learned patience at great cost. The trial and error of life among human beings had taught him that whenever a bunch of them began to jump up and down and shout at cross-purposes, the only thing a sane man could do was sit back and let them sort it out for themselves. No matter how long it took. The alternative was to try to attract their attention, either with explanations of the misunderstanding or with a return to the original topic of conversation, and to make that attempt meant that sooner or later you too would be jumping up and down and shouting at cross-purposes. Patience, patience; at the very worst, they would finally wear themselves out.

(Donald E. Westlake, *Bank Shot*)

trial and error: learning by making mistakes   *bunch:* group
at cross-purposes: misunderstanding each other   *sane:* opposite of mad

---

(*Punch*)

"Daddy and I have no need of drugs. That's because Daddy and I lead full, rich lives."

Bringing up children

[Extract from an interview.]

'One reason why the family unit is crumbling is that parents have relinquished their authority over children. The permissive school of thought says "Let the child do what he wants to when he wants to, no matter what it is, don't warp his personality, don't thwart him, you'll ruin him for life". Because of this we've got a generation of spoilt self-centred brats with no respect for their elders. Children always push to see how much they can get away with; if you give them nothing to push against, there are no moral limits, no moral convictions will develop in the children. We have this in the schools – children have much less respect for their teachers nowadays.'

How do you define respect?

'Realising that someone else might have desires also. Respect doesn't mean that when someone in authority says "jump" you jump – that's the military approach – but young people today, if they have an opinion that's different from yours, then you're the fool and they're right, even if they don't have enough experience to judge.'

How do you feel about children using swearwords?

'I never hear them swear, but I saw one of my daughter's diaries once, and it was full of a word that I'd have spanked her for if she'd said it aloud. Swearing goes against my sensibilities. It's mental laziness. If people aren't allowed to swear they use their brains to find a better word.'

Do you think it's just a matter of convention or do you think there's a deeper moral objection to swearing?

'I think it's not done. It's taboo in nice society. We've been taught not to swear, and I think well-brought-up people should avoid it. If I ever hear a woman use "s-h-i-t" I think a lot less of them.'   (Margaret, 43, American)

crumbling: breaking to pieces
relinquished: given up
school of thought: group of people who think the same way
warp: twist
thwart him: oppose his wishes, frustrate him
brats: unpleasant children
swearwords: 'bad' words
spanked: smacked, hit
convention: custom

The stern parent

Father heard his children scream,
So he threw them in the stream,
Saying, as he drowned the third,
'Children should be seen, *not* heard'.

(Harry Graham, *Most Ruthless Rhymes*)

"Listen mate! I didn't ask to be born but since you brought me into this mess the least you can do is stuff me full of sweets."

mate: friend

The proper time to influence the character of a child is about a hundred years before he is born.

Dean Inge

Baby and child care

HE ISN'T FRAIL. 'I'm so afraid I'll hurt him if I don't handle him right,' a mother often says about her first baby. You don't have to worry; you have a pretty tough baby. There are many ways to hold him. If his head drops backward by mistake, it won't hurt him. The open spot in his skull (the fontanel) is covered by a tough membrane like canvas that isn't easily injured. The system to control his body temperature is working quite well by the time he weighs 7 pounds if he's clothed sensibly. He has good resistance to most germs. During a family cold epidemic, he's apt to have it the mildest of all.

A FATHER SHOULD GO LIGHT ON TEASING. On the average, men seem to have more fierceness in them than women do. In civilized life, they have to keep this under control. When a man feels irritated at a friend or a business associate, he can't simply hit him or insult him. But according to the rules, it's all right to kid him a little. So men learn to be kidders. Then when a father feels mildly irritated at his son, he may try to work it off as kidding. A child feels humiliated when he's laughed at, and he doesn't know how to tease back. Teasing is too strong for young children.

TEMPER TANTRUMS. Almost any baby has a few temper tantrums between 1 and 3 years. He's developed a sense of his own desires and individuality. When he's thwarted he knows it and feels angry. Yet he doesn't usually attack the parent who has interfered with him. Perhaps the grown-up is too important and too big. Also, his fighting instinct isn't very well developed yet.

When the feeling of fury boils up in him, he can't think of anything better to do than take it out on the floor and himself. He flops down, yelling, and pounds with his hands and feet and maybe his head.

A temper tantrum once in a while doesn't mean anything; there are bound to be some frustrations. If they are happening regularly, several times a day, it may mean that the child is getting overtired or has some chronic physical trouble.

It's embarrassing to have a child put on a tantrum on a busy pavement. Pick him up, with a grin if you can force it, and lug him off to a quiet spot where you can both cool off in private.

Dr Spock

---

frail: fragile, delicate
germs: microbes
apt: likely
mildest: least seriously
teasing: laughing at people, aggressive joking
kid: tease

fury: very strong anger
flops down: falls down
yelling: shouting
pounds: hits
chronic: long-lasting
lug: (slang) pull

Spock's guide to parent care

PARENTS ARE JUST LARGE HUMAN BEINGS. It's only natural for a small child to feel a little daunted by the hard work and responsibility of coping with parents. All parents get balky from time to time, and go through phases which worry their children, and all children get tired and discouraged and wonder whether they're doing the right thing.

The important thing to remember is that most parents, deep down inside, want nothing more than to be good ones. A parent may act tough and cocky, but at heart he wants to be one of the gang. He wants to learn what's expected of him as a parent and do it. What he needs from you above all is plenty of encouragement, and plenty of reassurance that he's doing all right.

EVERY PARENT IS DIFFERENT. This one flies into a fury at the sight of crayoning on the wallpaper. That one bursts into tears. Yet another goes into a sulk and won't say anything all afternoon. All these are perfectly normal, healthy reactions. I'd be inclined to be suspicious of the parent who seems a little too good to be true. He or she may be deprived of emotional experience for lack of opportunity. I think I'd ask myself in this case if I was drawing on the wallpaper enough.

THEY AREN'T AS FRAGILE AS THEY LOOK. Handle them confidently. Many parents look as though they'll have a nervous breakdown if you bang your toy on the table just once more. Don't worry – nine times out of ten they won't.

TEMPER TANTRUMS. Almost all parents have temper tantrums from time to time. You have to remember that between the ages of 20 and 60 parents are going through a difficult phase of their development. They have got to a stage in their exploration of the world at which they find it is rather smaller than they thought. They are discovering the surprising limitations of their personality, and learning to be dependent. It's natural enough for them to want to explode at times.

It's no use arguing with a parent who's in this sort of state. The best thing is just to let him cool off. But you might try to distract him and offer him a graceful way out by suggesting something that's fun to do, like taking it out of your little brother instead.

GO EASY ON KIDDING. Most parents enjoy a joke. If you get hold of a good one, try it on them 20 or 30 times, just to show them what it's like being on the receiving end of the family's sense of humour. But I think I'd give it a rest after that, in case it causes nightmares.

REMEMBER, YOU'RE HELPING THEM TO GROW UP. It's your job to help your parents grow up into mature, responsible old-age pensioners, self-confident, armed with a workable code of morals and manners, and too exhausted in mind and body to make trouble for anyone else. If you keep in mind that you're training your children's grandparents you won't go far wrong.

Michael Frayn

daunted: discouraged   *cocky:* superior
balky: unco-operative   *sulk:* quiet rage

"Hello, Dr. Spock. Say, I hate to bother
you, but I've got this Forty-year-old kid."

(Punch)

"George simply loves playing with the children."

(*Daily Mirror*)

Naughtiness seen as stress sign in children

Abnormally aggressive or submissive behaviour in a child is often a cry for help and should be treated with support and understanding, not with criticism and punishment, a psychologist says.

Writing in the latest edition of **Where**, an education magazine for parents, published today, Mr James Hemming urges parents and teachers to look out for the stress signals displayed by children when they are unhappy or worried but do not want to admit it.

He says that crises and setbacks are good for a child if he has the capacity and adult support to cope with them. But if tney are beyond him his confidence may be sapped and he may go into a nervous retreat or become untypically aggressive.

Children under stress cover up their difficulties for reasons of self-esteem or anxiety to live up to parents' expectations.

They may be competing with older brothers and sisters and will go to great lengths to "prove" they are not inferior. Or they may fear the ridicule of their peers.

Mr Hemming sees regression as a typical stress signal. The child takes a step back in the growing-up process, and, for example, may start to wet his bed again. A sudden decline in confidence lasting beyond a mere mood is likely to be linked with a deep discouragement.

Stealing, other than exporatory and adventure stealing found among boys of about eight, usually indicates an emotional lack and is a symbolic attempt to make up for it.

Children who feel physically interior often give stress signals. Bullying is a common sign and should be treated sympathetically. The bully who is punished merely learns to be more careful.

An unexpected decline in general competence is a stress signal that may accompany too little success in relation to others. The child says to himself: " I'm no good, so what's the point in trying ? "

" Failure is like strychnine ", Mr Hemming writes. "A little can be a stimulant, a little more than a little is a poison." If a child, normally eager to talk about what he is doing at school, suddenly clams up it is very likely that he has hit a bad patch.

Mounting obstinacy is often an indication of difficult relations with others. It may grow from a sense of being dominated by someone, or it may be a way of self-expression for a lonely and defeated child. The best counter to obstinacy, as to many awkward attitudes, is plenty of appreciation.

In dealing with stress signals, Mr Hemming urges parents to distinguish between support and intervention. Children always welcome support, but may resent intervention. Only when support has failed shoul dtactful intervention be used. Criticism increases stress and undesirable behaviour.

One way to counteract a child's reticence to talk about his worries and fears is for parents to share their own difficulties with their children.

(Diana Geddes in *The Times*)

stress: nervous tension
submissive: allowing oneself to be dominated
setbacks: difficulties, discouragements
sapped: weakened
self-esteem: good opinion of themselves
their peers: children in the same age-group
regression: babyish behaviour
decline: reduction
bullying: aggressive behaviour towards other children
competence: ability
strychnine: a drug
clams up: becomes silent
hit a bad patch: started a bad period
obstinacy: refusal to do what others want
counter: answer

Why did the children

Why did the children
put beans in their ears
when the one thing we told the children
they must not do
was put beans in their ears?

Why did the children
pour molasses on the cat
when the one thing we told the children
they must not do
was pour molasses on the cat?

Carl Sandburg

molasses: thick dark syrup produced during sugar manufacture

You can't push your grandmother off a bus

Quickly

Oh ye cannae shove yer granny aff a bus
Ye cannae shove yer granny aff a bus
Ye cannae shove yer granny
Cause she's yer mammy's mammy
Ye cannae shove yer granny aff a bus.

Ye can shove yer other granny aff a bus
Ye can shove yer other granny aff a bus
Ye can shove yer other granny
Cause she's yer faither's mammy
Ye can shove yer other granny aff a bus.

(Scottish children's street song)

Pantomime Poem

'HE'S BEHIND YER!'
chorused the children
but the warning came too late.

The monster leaped forward
and fastening its teeth into his neck,
tore off the head.

The body fell to the floor
'MORE' cried the children

'MORE, MORE, MORE

MORE

MC

Roger McGough

Pantomime: theatrical performance for children (especially at Christmas)

Not mine

So you
want
to know
why
I
dig pot?

Because
this world ain't mine man!
I didn't make it,
I can't change it,
I want out of it.

Sheila R. aged 15

I dig pot: (slang) I like marijuana

"See? Isn't this more fun than sitting around smoking pot?"

(*Punch*)

pot: (slang) marijuana

A teenager's experience with drugs

[From an interview with David, 22.]

When I was 14, 15, 16, I got involved with lots of drugs: I went through LSD, speed, blues, hash. I was very emotional at the time because I had constant hassles with my mother (I have no father) and I left home a lot of times and stayed with friends who were on drugs. I remember the first acid I took, some chick just put it in my mouth and it really freaked me. I really got frightened but after a couple of times I enjoyed it. You know you get a nice high tripping on LSD – but after two years I realized I was doing myself in, mucking up my bones and killing my brain cells. Moreover I couldn't really hold down a job because I used to get very stoned at nighttime and I couldn't get up in the morning – so I got into stealing and had a lot of trouble with the police.

Now I'm out of it – I still smoke hash from time to time but just for relaxation. I live for the day and I'm very happy with life: I've got nice friends who like me for what I am (I don't have to lie any more!) and a nice job selling clothes. Life has got so much to give you! Just living from day to day and meeting people is wonderful! I work and eat and drink wine and learn things and other people learn things from me, that's enough to keep me happy!

I'm not sorry I've been through life the hard way and experienced a lot of nasty things because I think that's what makes me enjoy my present life so much! I really enjoy myself lots you know!

LSD: lysergic acid, a hallucinatory drug
speed: (slang) amphetamine drugs
blues: (slang) barbiturate drugs
hash: hashish (the same as marijuana)
hassles: disagreements, quarrels
acid: (slang) LSD
chick: (slang) girl
it really freaked me: (slang) it put me into a strange state of consciousness
high: (slang) pleasant state of consciousness resulting from drug-taking
tripping: (slang) experiencing the effects of drugs
doing myself in: (slang) damaging myself
mucking up: (slang) damaging
stoned: (slang) affected by drugs

Red-Indian view of education

At the treaty of Lancaster, in Pennsylvania, anno 1744, between the Government of Virginia and the Six Nations, the commissioners from Virginia acquainted the Indians by a speech, that there was at Williamsburg a college with a fund for educating Indian youth; and that if the chiefs of the Six Nations would send down half a dozen of their sons to that college, the government would take care that they be well provided for, and instructed in all the learning of the white people.

The Indians' spokesman replied:

'We know that you highly esteem the kind of learning taught in those colleges, and that the maintenance of our young men, while with you, would be very expensive to you. We are convinced, therefore, that you mean to do us good by your proposal and we thank you heartily.

'But you, who are wise, must know that different nations have different conceptions of things; and you will not therefore take it amiss, if our ideas of this kind of education happen not to be the same with yours. We have had some experience of it; several of our young people were formerly brought up at the colleges of the northern provinces; they were instructed in all your sciences; but, when they came back to us, they were bad runners, ignorant of every means of living in the woods, unable to bear either cold or hunger, knew neither how to build a cabin, take a deer, nor kill an enemy, spoke our language imperfectly, were therefore neither fit for hunters, warriors nor counsellors; they were totally good for nothing.

'We are, however, not the less obligated by your kind offer, though we decline accepting it, and to show our grateful sense of it, if the gentlemen in Virginia will send us a dozen of their sons, we will take care of their education, instruct them in all we know, and make men of them.'

Benjamin Franklin

fund: provision of money
esteem: respect
maintenance: feeding, clothing, etc.
take it amiss: interpret it the wrong way
warriors: fighters
counsellors: advisers
obligated by: grateful for

The white man drew a small circle

The white man drew a small circle in the sand
and told the red man, 'This is what the Indian
knows,' and drawing a big circle around the
small one, 'This is what the white man knows.'
The Indian took the stick and swept an immense
ring around both circles: 'This is where the
white man and the red man know nothing.'

Carl Sandburg

Stagecoach

[This is an extract from the published film-script of John Ford's classic
Western *Stagecoach*. The text contains instructions for the actors and
cameraman as well as dialogue.]

A high angle very long shot looking over the desert shows the stagecoach
like a small toy pressing on alone through the desolate expanse towards
the mouth of a canyon. It is early evening. BUCK can be heard, off,
shouting at the horses. Suddenly, camera pans swiftly across to the rim
of the canyon wall to reveal a large band of savage-looking Apache
Indians, their foreheads smeared with white war-paint, lurking in
ambush, waiting for the stagecoach to enter the canyon below. At their
centre, looking down into the valley, stands the most dreaded figure in
the South-west, GERONIMO, powerful of frame, and with a craggy face
that seems to have been carved out of red rock.
Another Apache is seen close, with still others of the band on horseback
behind him.
Now GERONIMO is seen from below in front of a group of Apaches. One
of them points off.
The stagecoach is seen far away and below, as its horses gallop along in the
middle of the valley. There is little cover for miles around. Camera
swings round to the left and tilts up to the ridge to reveal the Apache
warband turning away. Most of those on horseback ride out of shot,
leaving GERONIMO and two or three of his warband standing and watching
them go.
Inside the coach the atmosphere is fairly relaxed and even GATEWOOD
makes an attempt at cheerfulness.
GATEWOOD: *Well, we'll soon be in Lordsburg. Sorry I flew off the handle,
Hatfield. Just nervous, you know how it is.* HATFIELD eyes him sardonically and

says nothing. *No hard feelings, I hope.*

PEACOCK sitting up, rather proud of himself: *Well, all in all, it's been an exciting ... Coughing ... but very interesting trip, now hasn't it?*

DOC BOONE looks up at him from his place on the floor of the coach.

DOC BOONE: *Well, now that the danger's past, Mister ...* PEACOCK looks down helpfully, while GATEWOOD looks on.

PEACOCK: *Er, Peacock.*

DOC BOONE off: *Ladies and gentlemen, since ...*

Cut back to DOC BOONE on the floor.

DOC BOONE: *... it's most unlikely that we'll ever have the pleasure of meeting again socially, I'd like to propose a toast.* He looks up, then takes the cork out of his bottle and looks at each of them in turn. *Major, Gatewood, Ringo ... Your health.*

HATFIELD off: *Thank you, sir.*

DOC BOONE takes a swig at the bottle, but as he does so there is a strange whistling sound and a thudding noise; DOC BOONE chokes on his bottle, looking up with his eyes wide in amazement. He looks round and camera pans swiftly left, now showing PEACOCK and GATEWOOD. PEACOCK has an arrow stuck in his shoulder. The little man is sitting bolt upright, a look of disbelief on his face. He utters no sound, as his right hand gropes to the arrow and holds it by the shaft, while blood pours down his hand. His face is frozen in agony for a moment, then, with a slight gurgle, he falls forward, watched in horror by GATEWOOD. Camera tilts down with him as he falls across DOC BOONE.

(John Ford and Dudley Nichols, *Stagecoach*)

high angle very long shot: instruction to the cameraman
canyon: deep cutting made by a river
pans: (cinema terminology) moves sideways
rim: edge
lurking in ambush: hiding ready to attack
dreaded: feared
Geronimo: a famous Apache Indian chief
craggy: rocky

tilts: points at an angle
I flew off the handle: I lost my temper
sardonically: with a critical smile
swig: swallow
bolt upright: very straight
gropes: moves unsteadily
shaft: straight part
agony: great pain
gurgle: liquid noise in the throat

Geronimo: the truth

[In his book *Bury my heart at Wounded Knee*, Dee Brown writes the history of the United States as seen 'from the West looking east' – that is to say, from the Indians' point of view. The picture he gives of Geronimo is rather different from the one usually found in Western stories and films.]

Geronimo later explained it this way: 'Sometime before I left, an Indian named Wadiskay had a talk with me. He said, "They are going to arrest you," but I paid no attention to him, knowing that I had done no wrong; and the wife of Mangas, Huera, told me that they were going to seize me and put me and Mangas in the guardhouse, and I learned from the American and Apache soldiers, from Chato, and Mickey Free, that the Americans were going to arrest me and hang me, and so I left.'

The flight of Geronimo's party across Arizona was a signal for an outpouring of wild rumours. Newspapers featured big headlines: THE APACHES ARE OUT! The very word 'Geronimo' became a cry for blood. The 'Tucson Ring' of contractors, seeing a chance for a profitable military campaign, called on General Crook to rush troops to protect defenseless white citizens from murderous Apaches. Geronimo, however, was desperately trying to avoid any confrontation with white citizens; all he wanted to do was speed his people across the border to the old Sierra Madre sanctuary.

[General Crook met Geronimo and persuaded him to surrender.]

'I give myself up to you,' Geronimo said. 'Do with me what you please. I surrender. Once I moved about like the wind. Now I surrender to you and that is all.'

[However, Geronimo believed that he was going to be betrayed and killed, and escaped again with his followers.]

'I feared treachery,' Geronimo said afterward, 'and when we became suspicious, we turned back.'

As a result of Geronimo's flight, the War Department severely reprimanded Crook for his negligence, for granting unauthorized surrender terms, and for his tolerant attitude towards Indians. He immediately resigned and was replaced by Nelson Miles (Bear Coat), a brigadier general eager for promotion.

Bear Coat took command on April 12, 1886. With full support from the War Department, he quickly put five thousand soldiers into the field (about one-third of the combat strength of the Army). He also had five hundred Apache scouts, and thousands of irregular civilian militia. He organized a flying column of cavalrymen and an expensive system of heliographs to flash messages back and forth across Arizona and New Mexico. The enemy to be subdued by this powerful military force was Geronimo and his 'army' of twenty-four warriors, who throughout the summer of 1886 were also under constant pursuit by thousands of soldiers of the Mexican Army.

(Dee Brown, *Bury my heart at Wounded Knee*)

contractors: suppliers of goods to the army
sanctuary: safe place
treachery: dishonest treatment, broken promises

reprimanded: criticized
unauthorized: not agreed by his superiors
combat: fighting

(*The Beezer*, a children's 'comic')

Gone west

I CAN SEE we're in for a pretty thin time when the new season's American television shows hit our screens. For a start, there's only one western among them and, take my word for it, that won't be much good.

No westerns are any good any more, since the psychologists and the Indians took over. In the old days you knew where you stood with a western : the villain had a black horse and a black hat and the hero had a white horse and a white hat and he was the one you cheered for, unless of course he turned out to be Roy Rogers and was so far lacking in normal human decency as to start singing at you, in which case you naturally cheered for the other bloke.

Not that it did you any good. Roy Rogers always won. I think it was all that singing that did it for him. It so shattered the villain's nerves that instead of going for his gun he put his hands over his ears, which left Roy Rogers still singing away during the final fade-out with one arm round Dale Evans and the other round Trigger, both of whom were happily tone deaf and didn't mind the noise.

However, Roy Rogers apart, you knew, as I said, where you stood. The hero was right and the heavy was wrong and that was that. But then psychology crept in, mixing the black with the white until you couldn't tell whether the hero was a heavy or the heavy was a hero. Take a film like High Plains Drifter in which Clint Eastwood breezed into town and slaughtered three men and had it away with the local whore before he'd even got off his horse or taken the cigar out of his mouth. Well, that can't be right, can it ? Worse than singing, that is. Gary Cooper never did things like that.

As for the **real** western, the cowboys and Injuns western, whatever happened to that ? You used to have thoroughly evil Injuns, rotten savages who went about their legitimate business of raping, pillaging and murdering in an admirably businesslike way, never pausing to clutter up the action with dialogue save for the obligatory 'Ugh' and 'Paleface speak with forked tongue.'

All that changed when America developed a social conscience about the Injuns and these days if you get a Redskin in a western at all he's a grave, peaceful character, infinitely more dignified than any Paleface, and if he should be so provoked as to attack a wagon train you know perfectly well that he's doing it more in sorrow than in anger and anyway the wagon train had it coming.

(Barry Norman, *Guardian*)

gone west: a play on words – the expression can mean disappeared or dead
in for: going to have
bloke: (slang) man
fade-out: the moment at the end of a film when the picture gradually disappears
Trigger: Roy Rogers' horse
the heavy: the bad man
breezed: came casually
slaughtered: killed
had it away with: had sex with
whore: prostitute
Injuns: Indians
pillaging: robbing
clutter up: litter
save for: except for
had it coming: deserved it

Make New Friends!
GO WEST
With General Custer's
7th CAVALRY

(*Mad Magazine*)

Fight with an Indian

I kicked my stool back and stood up and jerked the gun out of the holster under my arm. But it was no good. My coat was buttoned and I was too slow. I'd have been too slow anyway, if it came to shooting anybody.

There was a soundless rush of air and an earthy smell. In the complete darkness the Indian hit me from behind and pinned my arms to my sides. He started to lift me. I could have got the gun out still and fanned the room with blind shots, but I was a long way from friends. It didn't seem as if there was any point in it.

I let go of the gun and took hold of his wrists. They were greasy and hard to hold. The Indian breathed gutturally and set me down with a jar that lifted the top of my head. He had my wrists now, instead of me having his. He twisted them behind me fast and a knee like a corner stone went into my back. He bent me. I can be bent. I'm not the City Hall. He bent me.

I tried to yell, for no reason at all. Breath panted in my throat and couldn't get out. The Indian threw me sideways and got a body scissors on me as I fell. He had me in a barrel. His hands went to my neck. Sometimes I wake up in the night. I feel them there and I smell the smell of him. I feel the breath fighting and losing and the greasy fingers digging in. Then I get up and take a drink and turn the radio on.

(Raymond Chandler, *Farewell my lovely*)

gutturally: with a throaty noise
jar: jerk
scissors: a wrestling hold in which one fighter gets both legs round the other
he had me in a barrel: (slang) I was helpless

Waking up

The first sensation was that if anybody spoke harshly to me I should burst out crying. The second that the room was too small for my head. The front of the head was a long way from the back, the sides were an enormous distance apart, in spite of which a dull throbbing beat from temple to temple. Distance means nothing nowadays.

The third sensation was that somewhere not far off an insistent whining noise went on. The fourth and last was that ice water was running down my back. The cover of a day bed proved that I had been lying on my face, if I still had one. I rolled over gently and sat up and a rattling noise ended in a thump. What rattled and thumped was a knotted towel full of melting ice cubes. Somebody who loved me very much had put them on the back of my head. Somebody who loved me less had bashed in the back of my skull. It could have been the same person. People have moods.

(Raymond Chandler, *Playback*)

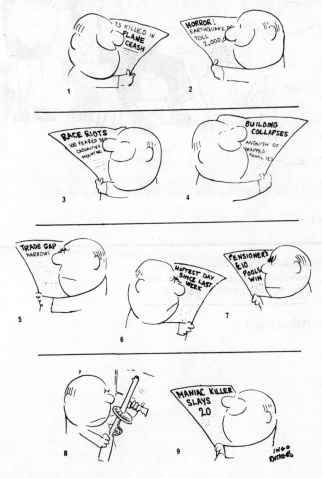

"Very clever, but I've made the apple-sauce. Kill it!"

(*Punch*)

WANTED – man and woman to look
after two cows, both Protestant.

(Ulster paper)

Song of the battery hen

We can't grumble about accommodation:
we have a new concrete floor that's
always dry, four walls that are
painted white, and a sheet-iron roof
the rain drums on. A fan blows warm air
beneath our feet to disperse the smell
of chicken-shit and, on dull days,
fluorescent lighting sees us.

You can tell me: if you come by
the North door, I am in the twelfth pen
on the left-hand side of the third row
from the floor; and in that pen
I am usually the middle one of three.
But, even without directions, you'd
discover me. I have the same orange-
red comb, yellow beak and auburn
feathers, but as the door opens and you
hear above the electric fan a kind of
one-word wail, I am the one
who sounds loudest in my head.

Listen. Outside this house there's an
orchard with small moss-green apple
trees; beyond that, two fields of
cabbages; then, on the far side of
the road, a broiler house. Listen:
one cockerel grows out of there, as
tall and proud as the first hour of sun.
Sometimes I stop calling with the others
to listen, and wonder if he hears me.

The next time you come here, look for me.
Notice the way I sound inside my head.
God made us all quite differently,
and blessed us with this expensive home.

Edwin Brock

battery hen: hen kept shut up, unable to move freely
grumble: complain
you can tell me: you can recognize me
comb: the red ridge of flesh on top of a hen's head

auburn: reddish-brown
wail: complaining noise
broiler: bird kept in battery
cockerel: male bird

Colonel Sir Lancelot Rolleston, D.S.O, a well-known Nottinghamshire fox-hunter and a former master of hounds, says: 'If foxes, like women, had a vote, I think they would vote unanimously for the keeping up of fox-hunting. I have known a fox that was absolutely devoted to fox-hunting . . . after we had hunted him many seasons, I regret to say we killed him.'

(*Daily Mail*)

hounds: hunting dogs
unanimously: in complete agreement

Out with the Hunt

Now here we are in the heart of Britain's countryside on a cold and crisp wintry morning waiting for the Shepherds Bush Foxhunt to come by. I can't see or hear them yet so to pass the time I'll describe the picturesque scenery in front of me. It's a typical English countryside scene. In the foreground are rich fertile fields and a winding stream which sparkles under the wintry sun; in the background, a row of majestic looking hills. Behind me is a quaint old English farm, from which comes the sound of churns rattling and pigs squealing. Yes indeed it is true to say that the air is alive with the sounds and smells of the countryside and I can hear the farmer quietly laughing and drooling as he counts his subsidies.

But here comes the hunt, yes, here they come now and what a splendid sight they make as they trample nonchalantly across a field of young Spring wheat . . . tally ho, tally ho!

They're right in front of me now and they all look as though they have their hearts set on a kill today. Yes indeed, what a magnificent sight with the huntsmen in immaculate scarlet and the women in bowler hats and jodhpurs, a typically English sight to warm the heart!

We watch them now as they jump over the dyke into a field of sugarbeet, all except one that is, who has parted company from his mount which has galloped off and left him. But he's all right. At the moment he's sitting in the dyke up to his midriff in water and muttering, but as he's unhurt we'll move on quickly to catch up with the remainder of the . . . hallo, that's funny . . . er, my attention has just been drawn to the fact that there are a number of foxes charging down the hillside from the wood on my right. Yes, there must be at least twenty of them, indeed a unique sight. What can they be after I wonder?

Oh dear, they've spotted the huntsman without a hunt and, judging by his reactions, he's spotted them. Indeed it's a most intriguing scene before me now as the petrified huntsman runs for his life pursued by the pack of snarling foxes. The foxes are now only about one hundred yards away from him and gaining extremely quickly. I doubt very much if he will be able to outrun them or indeed outwit them, although he's trying gallantly, but I'm afraid he appears to be tiring rapidly and, my word! he's collapsed in a field of spinach. From where I'm sitting it looks as though he's caught his foot in a gin trap. Yes he has, I'm afraid. Oh, I say, what bad luck!

He hasn't got a chance of escape now and the leading foxes have almost got him. He's trying gallantly to shoo them away and is waving his braces at them, but I'm afraid it's too late now and they've got him.

The foxes are now snapping and biting viciously at his neck and limbs and a tug-of-war has developed and the foxes are pulling and tearing away at the body but he's still alive. Yes, I can definitely hear him screaming.

I must say that it's a most interesting scene before me, not exactly what I had hoped to see, but nevertheless extremely interesting. The screaming has stopped now and I think he must be dead.

Now what's happening? Oh yes, I see they're carrying out the ceremony of 'blooding', in which the faces of the young fox cubs are smeared with the scalp of the prey, a fascinating custom.

There's a commotion going on on my left where a group of foxes have just arrived carrying banners and placards to protest over the kill. They seem to regard the sport as barbaric!

I'll leave you now with the words of the Master of Fox Hounds who told me before the hunt commenced that he firmly believed that the fox enjoyed the hunt just as much as the huntsmen. I think he may be right.

Bryan McAllister, aged 17

Ronald Searle.

"Oh! Sorry, Sir."

Oswald the seal

When I first noticed Oswald (as we christened him) he was busily engaged in stalking a long ribbon of glittering green seaweed that lay on the shingle, and which he was obviously under the impression was some sort of monstrous sea-serpent which was threatening the colony. He shambled towards it, bleary-eyed, and stopped a yard or so away to sniff. A slight wind twitched the end of the seaweed, and at this obviously threatening display Oswald turned and lolloped off as fast as his flippers would carry him. He stopped a safe distance away and peered over his shoulder, but the wind had died now and the seaweed lay still. Carefully he approached it again, stopping some six feet away to sniff, his fat little body taut and trembling, ready to run should he see the slightest movement. But the seaweed lay quiet in the sun, shining like a ribbon of jade. He approached it slowly and carefully, giving the impression that he was almost tiptoeing on his great flat flippers, and holding his breath in case of accidents. Still the seaweed made no movement. Cheered by this display of cowardice, Oswald decided that it was his duty to save the colony from this obviously dangerous enemy, which was liable to take them unawares. He shuffled his bottom to and fro ridiculously, so that his hind flippers got a good grip in the shingle, and then launched himself at the seaweed. In his enthusiasm he rather overshot the mark, and ended up on his nose in a fountain of shingle, but with a large section of the seaweed firmly grasped in his mouth. He sat up, the seaweed dangling from either side of his mouth like a green moustache, looking very pleased that his first bite had apparently disabled the enemy completely. He shook his head from side to side, making the weed flap to and fro, and then, shambling to his flippers, he galloped off along the beach trailing the weed on each side of him, occasionally shaking his head vigorously, as if to make sure his victim was really dead. For a quarter of an hour he played with the weed, until there was nothing left but a few tattered remnants. Then he flung himself down on the shingle, exhausted, the remains of the weed wound round his tummy like a cummerbund, and sank into a deep sleep.

Gerald Durrell

seal: animal that lives in the sea
christened: named
stalking: moving carefully to attack
shingle: stony beach
sea-serpent: imaginary snake-like sea-monster
colony: family of seals
shambled: moved unsteadily
bleary-eyed: sleepy-eyed
sniff: smell
lolloped: ran
flippers: a seal's feet
taut: tense
take them unawares: take them by surprise
shuffled: moved from side to side
hind: back
vigorously: energetically
tattered: torn to pieces
tummy: child's word for stomach
cummerbund: wide coloured ribbon worn round the stomach

'All Right, Have It Your Way – You Heard a Seal Bark'

The Loch Ness monster's song

Sssnnnwhufffll?
Hnwhuffl hhnnwfl hnfl hfl?
Gdroblboblhobngbl gbl gl g g g g glbgl.
Drublhaflablhaflubhafgabhaflhafl fl fl –
gm grawwwww grf grawf awfgm graw gin.
Hovoplodok-doplodovok-plovodokot-doplodokosh?
Splgraw fok fok splgraf hatchgabrlgabrl fok splfok!
Zgra kra gka fok!
Grof grawff gahf?
Gombl mbl bl –
blm plm,
blm plm,
blm, plm,
blp.

Edwin Morgan

Science report

Palaeontology: Speed of dinosaurs

In the face of recent suggestions that dinosaurs may have been livelier beasts than tradition suggests, Professor Alexander of Leeds University, has done some ingenious calculations which tend to restore their traditional lumbering image. The conventional view has been challenged both by the publication of Adrian Desmond's controversial book, *The Hotblooded Dinosaurs,* and by recent pictorial reconstructions showing the enormous reptiles galloping full tilt across the Jurassic plains. But Professor Alexander has taken measures of the dinosaurs' strides from their fossilized footprints, and by applying a modified version of a calculation originally designed for estimating the speed of ships, he has arrived at the conclusion that the larger dinosaurs were slow-moving beasts which seldom, if ever, ran.

Professor Alexander's calculations depend on the fact that there is a definite mathematical relationship between speed, leg length and length of stride. But to arrive at that formula he had first to collect empirical data from a large number of living animal species, including horses, elephants, jirds (rodent rather like gerbils), ostriches, and his own two children, aged 11 and 13, who ran over 25 metres of sandy beach last Christmas Eve so that he could make measurements on their footprints.

The mathematical relationship, which turned out to be the same for all those diverse species, is known as the Froude number. By taking measurements of leg length from skeletal remains, and stride length from fossilized footprints, and then using the Froude number, Professor Alexander was able to calculate the speed of six species of two-legged dinosaurs and two species of sauropod.

Mammals, according to Professor Alexander, do not usually break into a run or trot until the Froude number reaches a specific value (0.6) and the stride length is twice the leg length. According to those criteria, only two of the smaller dinosaur species investigated by Professor Alexander ran; or only two of them were running at the time they made their fossilized tracks.

It is possible that the larger species may have moved faster at other times, leaving no record to prove it. But Professor Alexander took measurements from more than one specimen of the same species in several cases, and he found that the speeds were similar each time. That implies that the speeds he has calculated were characteristic, and that large dinosaurs moved quite as slowly as one might expect of an animal in which it might take a nerve impulse as much as 10 seconds to travel from head to leg.

(The Times)

---

palaeontology: the study of old forms of life
dinosaurs: large reptiles that lived millions of years ago
ingenious: clever
lumbering: moving slowly and heavily
controversial: the subject of disagreement

full tilt: at top speed
Jurassic: period from about 200 million to about 140 million years ago
fossilized: preserved in stone
species: type of animal
implies: suggests

Tyrannosaurus Rex

It came on great oiled, resilient, striding legs. It towered thirty feet above half of the trees, a great evil god, folding its delicate watchmaker's claws close to its oily reptilian chest. Each lower leg was a piston, a thousand pounds of white bone, sunk in thick ropes of muscle, sheathed over in a gleam of pebbled skin like the mail of a terrible warrior. Each thigh was a ton of meat, ivory and steel mesh. And from that great breathing cage of the upper body those two delicate arms dangled out front, arms with hands which might pick up and examine men like toys, while the snake neck coiled. And the head itself, a ton of sculptured stone, lifted easily upon the sky. Its mouth gaped, exposing a fence of teeth like daggers. Its eyes rolled, ostrich eggs, empty of all expression save hunger. It closed its mouth in a dead grin. It ran, its pelvic bones crushing aside trees and bushes, its taloned feet clawing damp earth, leaving prints six inches deep wherever it settled its weight. It ran with a gliding ballet step, far too poised and balanced for its ten tons. It moved into a sunlit arena warily, its beautifully reptile hands feeling the air.

Ray Bradbury

Tyrannosaurus Rex: a dinosaur
resilient: springy
piston: cylinder which transmits power in an engine
sheathed: covered
mail: metal clothing
mesh: net
gaped: opened wide
daggers: knives
pelvic bones: the pelvis is the bony structure which connects the legs to the body
taloned: with claws
poised: the same as *balanced*
arena: open space for fighting

'My God –
Roget's Thesaurus!'

Roget's Thesaurus: despite the appearance of the name, this is not a dinosaur, but a well-known dictionary of synonyms

211

..., customa,
.rming, conventiona.
.rmable.

82. Multiformity – N. *multiformity,*
heterogeneity, variety, diversity 17 n.
non-uniformity; multifariousness, many-
sidedness, polymorphism; variability
152 n. *changeableness*, 604 n. *caprice*;
all-rounder; Proteus, Jekyll and Hyde;
kaleidoscope.

(Roget's Thesaurus)

Index

Topics

Poems and songs

Cartoons